INCREDIBLE
GOLF
STORIES

INCREDIBLE GOLF STORIES

AMAZING TALES FROM THE GREEN

EDITED BY JULIE GANZ

Skyhorse Publishing

Skyhorse Publishing books may be purchased in bulk at special discounts for sales promotion, corporate gifts, fund-raising, or educational purposes. Special editions can also be created to specifications. For details, contact the Special Sales Department, Skyhorse Publishing, 307 West 36th Street, 11th Floor, New York, NY 10018 or info@skyhorsepublishing.com.

Skyhorse® and Skyhorse Publishing® is are registered trademarks of Skyhorse Publishing, Inc.®, a Delaware corporation.

Visit our website at www.skyhorsepublishing.com.

10 9 8 7 6 5 4 3 2 1

Library of Congress Cataloging-in-Publication Data is available on file.

Cover design by Tom Lau
Cover photo credit AP Images

Print ISBN: 978-1-5107-1379-6
Ebook ISBN: 978-1-5107-1384-0

Printed in China

TABLE OF CONTENTS

INTRODUCTION

Discovery. Escape. Competition. Companionship. Growth. Change. Firsts and Lasts. Love. These are all aspects of the game of golf, and these themes are all evident in the stories that follow.

I can relate. It was a hot New York City afternoon in late July 2015, and my then-fiancé and I were heading out to the driving range at Chelsea Piers, an outing we hadn't yet taken together and one that we were very much looking forward to. After all, it had been an eventful but challenging summer. In the course of the last eight weeks, we had worked tirelessly on finalizing the details of our wedding, which at this point was a mere two months away; we had traveled to several out-of-town (most of which were actually out of state) weddings of friends and family; and my fiancé had completed law school and sat for the Bar exam. They were all positive changes, for sure, but changes that had kept us quite busy nonetheless.

It was for that reason and many others that the scenic driving range, with its views of the glistening Hudson River, seemed to beckon us. When we'd initially decided on the activity for the day, I'd felt a bit guilty—guilty for being away from it all, albeit for a few hours, to focus instead on the clubs, the golf balls, and the miraculous summer day that it was, rather than schedules, textbooks, and even floral arrangements. It's amazing how, with one swing of the golf club, outdoor recreation became a part of our lives again. Summer had truly begun for us that day, albeit over a month late.

In this escape from reality, we discovered that we still had some sense of hand-eye coordination. We regained a sense of competition and remembered that companionship didn't just mean working alongside each other on invitation stuffing or table charts. I loved my partner a little bit more with each piece of advice that he gave me about which club to use or how to drive that ball just a little bit farther—or straighter.

Of course, we didn't realize the significance of this rather spontaneous outing at the time, a quick release of energy before getting back to the plans and the details. In fact, the only real "change" I'd felt that next day was the soreness in my muscles, reminding me that I needed to exercise those limbs with at least as much frequency as I had been exercising my organizational skills. Yet, as the saying goes, hindsight is 20–20, and when I look back and reflect on that afternoon at the driving range, I realize just how much of an impact it actually had as we closed one chapter on our life and prepared for the next.

Golf can be reflective like that, if you let it be, sometimes eliciting feelings that you didn't even know existed. I hope that the classic tales and images that follow allow you to do the same. Though some are steeped more deeply in reality than others, I hope that at least some of them cause you to do some reflecting on your own golf experiences and remind you what it is you love about the game.

—Julie Ganz, Summer 2016

PART ONE

HISTORY

CHAPTER 1

HOW I BECAME THE FIRST FOREIGNER IN THE MODERN ERA TO WIN THE US OPEN

GARY PLAYER

Foreigners just didn't win the US Open in the modern era. Harry Vardon did it in 1900, becoming the first non-American to win. Ted Ray also achieved the feat in 1920. But it eluded South Africa's Bobby Locke, and he told me it was the one thing missing from his amazing career.

Of course, I wasn't immune to the aura of the US Open either. It had long been in my mind to win the US Open. But let's face it, American golfers dominated their national Open.

And of course, there was another not-so-small matter hanging in the balance here as well. The "Big Three"—the collective term for the dominance of myself, Arnold Palmer, and Jack Nicklaus—was now an established fact in the game. Between us we have won nearly sixty Majors on both the PGA and Senior (now Champions) Tours. This has never happened before by any three players and may never happen again.

By 1965, each of us had won three of the four Majors in the game. For Arnold, the PGA Championship was proving the elusive title. For Jack, it was the British Open. And for me, the US Open. I'd come close in 1958, finishing as runner-up four strokes behind Tommy Bolt.

So it came to pass that on a sweltering week in Missouri, in what is considered one of the most searching and demanding tests of golf established by

Harry Vardon became the first non-American golfer to win the US Open, which he accomplished in 1900. *(By Man vyi, via Wikimedia Commons)*

the United States Golf Association (USGA), the Grand Slam was beckoning. And for a foreigner on top of it.

As always, I did my homework. Ben Hogan was a master of the US Open, and he always arrived well before the tournament to get used to the local conditions. Like Hogan, I made sure I had my daily routine running smoothly, down to the finest detail. I didn't go out for dinner and stayed in my hotel room at night. I'm not a superstitious person, but I washed my same black golf shirt after every round and wore the same outfit every day.

Then I studied the golf course. It was a monster. At 7,190 yards it was the longest of any US Open golf course in history at that time, and was made even longer by the lousy equipment and balls we had. During the practice rounds, I made copious notes and sketches of the course and greens, and would then study them in my hotel room in the evenings.

I started off well by shooting an opening round 70 and was two shots off the lead of Australian Kel Nagle. I added another 70 in the second round and led Nagle by one stroke. A 71 in the third round kept me in front. It came down to the final nine holes, and what was now just a battle between Nagle and me. I was three strokes ahead of him to start the round.

Gary Player celebrates a successful putt during the second round of the 1965 US Open. *(AP Photo)*

Kel played superbly over those closing holes, cutting my lead down to only one stroke before I again opened up a three-stroke lead with three holes to play.

I stepped onto the tee at the par-three 16th. It's a long hole, and I had a three wood in my hands. But then the wind died suddenly. I changed to a four wood, but in my mind I had this thought that I need to hit it quickly before the next gust of wind came up again. It was a classic example of how impatience can cost you.

My ball finished in a plugged lie in the greenside bunker, and I made five. Kel had made three, cutting my lead to one again. And when Kel birdied the 17th, it vanished completely. We ended regulation play tied for the lead, setting up an 18-hole playoff on Monday.

I putted superbly in that playoff and was five up through the first eight holes on my way to winning the tournament with a 71 to Nagle's 74.

I had finally done it. I had won the US Open. I had won my first Major in a playoff. I had won the Grand Slam. I had become only the third person in history to win all four Majors, at the age of 29. I had followed in the footsteps of Gene Sarazen and Ben Hogan. And more significantly, I was the first foreigner to accomplish the feat. Forty-five years later, I remain the only one to do so.

I was also the first of "The Big Three" to reach this milestone. I particularly wanted to beat Jack Nicklaus to winning the Grand Slam. And Jack was a great sport about it. He urged me to practice with him the week before this Major rather than play in another tournament in St Louis. I told him I couldn't because I needed the money from another tournament in Greensboro, North Carolina, but he persisted and played a part in me winning the Grand Slam before him.

From a young age, when I first turned professional, winning the Grand Slam was something I always wanted to achieve. I'd read about Sarazen and Hogan having done it, and Bobby Jones winning his own amateur Grand Slam.

It was a great moment in my life, and I'm honored and grateful to have achieved it. No man does this on his own. It is merely a talent that is loaned to you. We have seen this talent taken away from many golfers, whether permanently or for a while: Ian Baker-Finch, Tom Watson, and David Duval, to name a few.

CHAPTER 2

MASTERS WEEK
AT AUGUSTA NATIONAL

TRIPP BOWDEN

It's the first full week in April, Masters Week, and I'm sitting on a bench in the caddy house, lacing up a pair of fresh-out-of-the box green-and-white FootJoys. The shoes are custom-made for Augusta National, caddies in particular.

This is the first year someone who's not a caddy gets the privilege of slipping them on.

That someone is me. Me and two others, a veteran Augusta caddy named Tip Lite and another kid who is a couple years older than me. I figure he must have some pull, though I never get around to asking how much.

Outside I retrace the cart steps from my ride with Freddie, and twenty minutes later I'm slipping under the yellow ropes and taking my position behind the 2nd green. The one Freddie drove onto from the Bobby Jones sundial wearing bedroom slippers.

It's a different sort of job, this forecaddying. My assignment is to fix players' ball marks and sweep sand off the green with a fiberglass pole after they blast out of the bunker. Sounds dull as Parcheesi at first glance, but I feel like the guy who feeds the dolphins at Sea World. It's a menial job, but once you're onstage, you get as many eyes on you as the Golden Bear himself.

There's no feeling quite like it, being not two feet from the likes of Nicklaus, Palmer, Player, and Watson, fixing their ball marks as they approach the green to raucous applause. Some players seem to appreciate us, some act as if we're not even there.

Palmer always says thank you.

Two years ago I had no idea who he was. Today I know him as the King. And the King just acknowledged one of his court jesters.

Good stuff, this. But as good as this is, it's not nearly as good as what awaits me after my job is done for the day.

Freddie's office.

Freddie's invited me to come by after I'm done, but only if I want to. My forecaddy ID gives me all-day and all-week access to Augusta National, the most revered golf course in the world. And to the Masters, the most elusive ticket in all of sports.

I understand if you want to take a rain check.

Rain check, my ass.

An invitation to Freddie's office blows everything else out of the water in ways you could never imagine. When the last group putts out I tell my fellow

Augusta National is the most revered golf course worldwide. *(AP Photo/Charlie Riedel)*

forecaddies I'll see 'em tomorrow. Walking toward the clubhouse, I repeat Freddie's words like a mantra.

Walk up to the pro shop like you belong. Push back your hat so the Pinkerton can see your eyes. Look dead into his and say, "I'm here to see Freddie." Don't miss a beat and don't slow down. Walk in like you own the place.

I do as I'm told, only to later realize all I ever need to do to access almost anything at Augusta is mention five simple words: *I'm here to see Freddie.*

After thanking the Pinkerton, I walk down the short path around the side of the pro shop, squeak open the door to Freddie's office. A tall, good-looking Spaniard is standing over Freddie's desk, talking in broken English. He would win the Masters that year, after a rain delay that pushed the tournament to Monday, beginning his final round 3, 3, 3.

Birdie, eagle, birdie.

Freddie sees me, nods, and flicks his wrist, the sign to come in. He gets up from his chair and gestures to it with an open hand and so I sit down. The Spaniard looks at me like I just walked on water. He turns to Freddie, asks about changing out his grips. Had Freddie ever done that before?

Freddie nods and says, "Yes, sir. All day long."

Under his breath I hear something else, but I can't quite make it out.

The Spaniard shakes Freddie's hand, thanks him, and leaves.

When the door bounces shut, Freddie opens his hand and a five-dollar bill falls onto the floor. He laughs.

"Ain't that something? That sonofabitch wants me to regrip his clubs and he gives me five bucks—*five bucks* to make sure they're ready for tomorrow!" He's really laughing now. "But I'll do it. Ain't no doubt about that." Freddie reaches into the Spaniard's bag and pulls out his driver. "Hey, this feels pretty good. Got it balanced just right."

The fiver is still lying on the floor.

He hands me the driver. I stand up, grip it, and waggle. I'm in awe as much as I am dumbfounded, but Freddie's right. This club feels great.

"So, how'd it go, man? You make out all right?"

"It was awesome," I say, and then I tell him how Chi Chi Rodriguez poked me with his putter and asked if I was Frank Beard's son (I had no idea who Frank Beard was) and how Arnold Palmer thanked me for fixing his ball mark. Looked me right in the eye.

"You mean this guy?" asks Freddie, in a voice only I can hear.

In walks the King himself.

"Hey, Freddie," says Palmer as the two men shake hands. "Always good to see you."

"Always good to be seen," says Freddie, "especially at my age." Palmer laughs, and they talk about things that don't pertain to me, don't pertain to golf. I stand there in pure disbelief, not three feet from the man who, through television and his amazing charisma, changed the game of golf forever.

Just like with the Spaniard, I can feel Arnie's eyes on me, wondering who I must be, given access to this mother of all backstage passes.

"This here's my doctor's son," says Freddie, as if reading Arnie's mind.

The look on his face says he has a vague memory of me, but nothing clicks. He smiles a hello, turns to Freddie, back to me, then Freddie again. He says something about him and his 4-iron no longer being friends, then pulls the iron out of the bag and grips it.

What a grip! If God had hands they would be Arnie's. Wrapped around a golf club they look like something off a wall in the Sistine Chapel. No wonder they call him the King.

Arnie slips the 4-iron back in the bag, tells Freddie he'll see him tomorrow, and walks out, waving as he goes.

"Check this out," says Freddie as the door shuts. He hands me Arnie's 4-iron. The clubface has his name on it. "Grip it, see what you think."

Are you kidding me? Grip Arnold Palmer's 4-iron?

But grip it I do, and the leather grip feels sticky and smells like earth. Not dirt, but the big ball you're standing on.

"This is real golf here, man. How the game was meant to be played. Leather grips, iron shafts, and a ball that won't fly to hell and gone." Freddie

Arnold Palmer, known as the King, always says thank you. *(AP Photo/Charlie Riedel)*

looks at me, looks through me, comes back to himself, and reaches for the 4-iron. "Come over here," he says. "Got something I want you to see."

What could possibly top this?

CHAPTER 3

MY JOURNEY TO AMERICA

HARRY VARDON

I was intent on making a bold bid for this American Open Championship. Victory in it seemed to be the one thing essential to make my trip the greatest possible success. My friend Taylor, who had just beaten me for the Open Championship at St. Andrews, had himself come over to the States and was also a candidate for the premier honours of American golf. As it turned out, we had practically the whole contest at Wheaton to ourselves, and a rare good duel it was, at the end of which I was at the top of the list, but only two strokes in front of my English opponent, while he was eight in front of the next man. The system of deciding the championship was the same as on this side, that is to say, four medal rounds were played, two on one day and two on the next. At the end of the first day's play I was just one stroke better than Taylor, my score for the two rounds being 157 to his 158, and on the second day I did 156 to his 157, so that on the whole event I was 313 to his 315. Taylor waited on the edge of the green while I holed out my last putt and was the first to grasp my hand in sincere congratulation. Beautiful weather, the biggest golfing crowd ever seen in America up to that time, and a good links made the tournament a great success. The partner who went round with me during this championship competition was Will Smith, the holder, who finished fifth.

I had some curious experiences in the course of my journeyings about the country, and I am not sure that they were all good for my game. During the early months I was down in Florida away from the cold and the snow.

I met some good golfers there. It was necessary to play an entirely different game from that to which we are accustomed in this country. There was no grass on the putting "greens." They were simply made of loose sand, sprinkled on the baked ground and watered and rolled. When there was a shortage of water and there was wind about, the fine part of the sand was blown away, and the surface of the "greens" then consisted of nothing but little pebbles. It was not easy to putt over this kind of thing, but I must not convey the impression that these sand "greens" were wholly bad. When properly attended to they are really nice to putt upon after you have become accustomed to them. It was impossible to pitch on to them, and one had to cultivate the habit of running up from a very long distance. Thus I got into the way of playing a kind of stab shot. The tees consisted not of grass but of hard soil, and one had to tee up much higher than usual in order to avoid damaging the sole of the driver. This provoked the habit of cocking the ball up, and as a corrective all the teeing grounds in Florida sloped upwards in front. Locusts were responsible for eating all the grass away from some courses, and I had a unique experience when I played Findlay at Portland. When we were on the putting greens, men had constantly to be beating sticks to keep the locusts off the lines of our putts. If it struck a locust the ball would come to a sudden stop. Acres and acres of land about there were without a single blade of grass. The locusts had eaten it all away. After we left Florida we reached some good courses, and resumed the old kind of play. It has often been suggested that the peculiar conditions of play in America, to which I was subjected for a long period, resulted in a permanent injury to my game as played at home, and in the light of reflection and experience I am persuaded to think that this is so. I have played well since then, have felt equal to doing anything that I ever did before, and have indeed won the Championship, but I think I left a very small fraction of my game in the United States.

In the way of other novel experiences I might mention that on one occasion I played as "Mr. Jones." I wanted a quiet day, and did not wish a too-attentive public to know where I was. Three friends joined me in a foursome, but when we went into the clubhouse after our game, another anxious golfer

Vardon may have left a part of his game behind when he went to play in the US. *(Carl Lindberg, via Wikimedia Commons)*

went up to my partner when I was standing by, and inquired of him whether he had heard that Vardon was playing on the links. My friend declared that he knew nothing of such a rumour, and I could hardly refrain from laughter as the anxious one went to pursue his inquiries in other quarters. Another time two other professionals and myself visited a course where we were unknown, and, hiding our identity, pretended that we were novices at the game, and begged of our caddies to advise us as to the best manner of playing each shot, which they did accordingly. We deliberately duffed most of our strokes at several holes, but this course of procedure tired us immensely, and so at last we abandoned it and began to play our natural game. Imagine the consternation and the indignation of those caddies! Each one of them threw down his bag of clubs, and, declining to carry them for another hole, walked sulkily off the course. On one occasion we camped out for the night on the links on which we were playing, and a very pleasant variation from the ordinary routine we found it.

The American newspapers, to which I have frequently referred, do their golf reporting very well. Their journalism may be "sensational" or whatever you like to call it, but the golfing section of it was usually interesting, ingenious, and very intelligent and reliable. On the occasion of one match in which I played, a paper gave up nearly the whole of one of its pages to a large panoramic view of the links. The flight of my ball and that of my opponent, and the places where they stopped after every stroke, from the first to the last, were accurately marked. Thus the whole game was illustrated in a single picture in a very effective manner. As was inevitable, I was sometimes victimised by interviewers who wrote "interviews" with me which I had never accorded, containing most amazing particulars about my methods and habits. Occasionally a reporter was turned on to describe a game when he knew nothing about golf, and then the results were sometimes amusing. One of these writers had it that I "carried away the green with my drive." Another said I "dropped dead at the hole." When playing at Washington against two opponents, I happened to beat bogey at the first hole. One of the reporters was told of this achievement, but did not quite understand it. Going to the next

A Vardon approach shot. *(USGA, via Wikimedia Commons)*

hole, we were walking through a bunker when he came up to me and politely inquired if that—the bunker—was the kind of bogey that I had beaten. I was told a very good story of American golf reporting. A match was arranged between two well-known amateurs, one of whom happened to be a very rich banker. One reporter, who admitted that he "knew nothing about the darned game," arrived rather late on the course, and borrowed the "copy" of an experienced golfing journalist for information of what had already happened. When this "copy" was duly returned with thanks, the late-comer remarked to his obliging friend, "Say, you made a bad mistake in one part." "What was it?" the other asked. "Waal, you say that So-and-so 'lipped the hole for a half.'" "Yes, that is right" "Oh, go away; you don't mean to tell me that a rich man like that would be playing for a paltry fifty cents. I've altered it to 'lipped the hole for a hundred dollars.'" And I remember that once when I was playing the best ball of two amateurs, one of the reporters had been instructed by his chief to keep the best ball score. I happened to lose the match on the last green, but on looking through the paper the next morning I was surprised to see it stated that I was beaten by not one but many holes, making this defeat in fact the biggest inflicted on me during my tour. The paper said that it was. I could not make anything out of it for some time, until at last I discovered that the reporter had reckoned my score also in the best ball figures! Obviously I could not beat myself. The best I could do was to get a half, and that was how it came about that I never won a single hole in the "Harry Vardon *v.* Harry Vardon and two others" match.

CHAPTER 4

MY FIRST NATIONAL CHAMPIONSHIP

FRANCIS OUIMET

The 1910 Amateur Championship at The Country Club, Brookline, where I saw Mr. Herreshoff make the drive above mentioned, was the first national event I ever entered, my age at the time being seventeen years. I did not qualify, but my failure did not make me feel very badly, considering all the circumstances. My total of 169 in the qualifying rounds was only one stroke worse than the top qualifying figure; and among those who, like myself, failed to get in the match play were such noted golfers as Robert A. Gardner, then the national amateur champion, and H. Chandler Egan, a former champion.

Furthermore, I played under circumstances that were a handicap in themselves. The championship field was inordinately large, and I was among the late starters for the first round, getting away from the first tee at 2:44 in the afternoon. This would have been ample time to get around before dark, had it not been for an extraordinary congestion at the third tee. Some one of the earlier starters was exceedingly slow, not to mention the time taken to search for a ball, and other little things that helped to cause delay and hold the players back. When my partner and I arrived at the third tee, there were ten pairs then waiting for an opportunity to play that hole, and there was nothing to do but wait. An hour and ten minutes of waiting at one tee in a championship is not conducive to best efforts; at any rate, it was not in my case.

Ouimet waited at the tee for over an hour, due to the high volume of golfers in the field. *(MarkHatfield, courtesy of iStock)*

While waiting at this tee, I remember having watched W. C. Chick take eight for the sixth hole, and, while mentally sympathizing with him, I did not dream that I would get a similar figure for my own card, when I finally did play the third hole, for I had started most satisfactorily with four for the first hole, and the same figure for the second. When it came my turn to drive from the third tee, I drove into a trap, lost a stroke getting out, put my third in the woods, was back on the fair green in four, on the green in five, and then took three putts for an eight. But from that point, I was forty-four strokes for the first nine holes. By this time, the afternoon was pretty well gone, and my partner and I had to stop playing at the fourteenth, because of darkness. As my card showed even fours for the first five holes of the inward half, I was beginning to feel better, and had I been able to complete the round that day, I think I might have been around in seventy-nine or eighty.

Along with several other pairs who were caught in the same dilemma, I had to go out the following morning to play the remaining four holes, and the best I could get for them was a total of nineteen strokes, whereas I would do those same holes ordinarily in sixteen strokes, at most. My score of eighty-three for the first round was not bad, however, and a similar round the second day would have put me in the match play.

But I had made one serious mistake, as I learned in the course of the second round. My supposition had been that, after playing the last four holes of the first round on the morning of the second day, I would have ample time to go home to breakfast and then return for the second round, my home being in close proximity to the grounds. What actually happened was that, after completing the four holes of the first round, I was told to report immediately at the first tee for my second round, in which I was to have the pleasure of being partnered with the then-president of the United States Golf Association, Robert C. Watson. For the first nine holes I had reason to feel satisfied, doing them in forty-one strokes, with every prospect of doing even better in the scoring for the last nine, which are less difficult. But by this time the pangs of hunger had taken a firm hold, and I could feel myself weakening physically, which was the result both of my failure to get breakfast, and the strain of a week of hard practising. The consequence was that I made a poor finish, took forty-five for the last nine, eighty-six for the round, and had one hundred and sixty-nine for my thirty-six-hole total, or just out of the match-play running. The moral is to be properly prepared for competition.

About that "week of hard practising" I would like to add a little. My experiences of practising for the championship of 1910 taught me a good lesson, which is that practising may easily be overdone. My idea of practising for that event was to get in at least thirty-six holes a day for the week prior to the championship. This was based partly on the idea that, with so much play, the game could be brought to such a point of mechanical precision that it would be second nature to hit the ball properly. The thought of "going stale" from so much play never occurred to me. Probably one reason was that I never had had a feeling of physical staleness in any sport up to that time. I always had been keen for golf, from the time of becoming interested in the game, and could not imagine a state of feeling that would mean even the slightest repugnance for play.

This is, perhaps, an error natural to youth and inexperience. It was not for me to know that a growing youth of seventeen years is not likely to have such a robust constitution that he can stand thirty-six holes of golf a day for a week, not to mention fairly steady play for weeks in advance of that, and still be on edge for a championship tournament.

It was not only on the Saturday previous to the championship (which began Monday) that I noticed this feeling of staleness. It did not come on all at once, by any means, and I did not realize what was the trouble, for on the day that I first noticed that I was not so keen for play as usual, I made a particularly good score. That day I was playing in company with H. H. Wilder, R. R. Freeman, and W. R. Tuckerman. This round was more or less of a tryout for places on the Massachusetts State team and I was fortunate enough to get in the best round, a seventy-six. Incidentally, I might add that this performance did not land me the coveted place on the State team, for Mr. Tuckerman reached the semifinals of the championship the succeeding week, which gave him precedence. That year I did play one match for the State team, however. It was in the match against Rhode Island, when the Massachusetts team found itself one man shy on the day set for play, which also was at The Country Club. Somebody discovered that I was in the vicinity, looked me up, and I played with a set of borrowed clubs, and also won my match.

To revert to the physical strain of too much practice, I found that on Saturday of the practice week my hands were sore, and than I was playing with unwonted effort, though not getting any better results than when hitting the ball with normal ease. It was my first lesson in the knowledge that when the game becomes a task, rather than a pleasure, something is wrong physically.

My advice to any golfer preparing for a championship is, therefore, not to overdo the practice end. To my mind, the wise thing is to play thirty-six holes a day for perhaps two days a week in advance of the championship. Then spend a morning in practising shots with the irons, the mashie, and putting, followed by a round of the course in the afternoon. This might be done for two or three days, with special attention given to the club which perhaps is not getting satisfactory results. One round of golf, without special exertion, the day before the tournament, after such a program, ought to put the player in good shape for the real competition. As for the superstition of some golfers that a particularly fine round in practice means so much less chance of duplicating it in tournament play, I hold a different view, which is that an especially good round gives an inspiration to equal it when the real test comes. I always feel after such a round that if I can do it once, there is no reason why I cannot again.

Elimination from the championship, in the qualifying round, had its compensations. It gave me the opportunity to watch the championship play for the remainder of the week, to see in action those golfers of whom I had heard so much. That in itself was a treat. Some of the matches, moreover, gave me some new ideas about golf as played in competition by men in the foremost ranks. For one thing, it was rather startling, if such a word can apply, to see a golfer like Mr. Herreshoff literally "swamped" in his match with Mr. Evans. Mr. Herreshoff had made the lowest score of the entire field in the qualifying round, yet here was the same man unable to put up anything but the most feeble opposition to the young Chicago golfer. Such a match only goes to show that the best of golfers occasionally have their bad days, days on which they find it seemingly impossible to play satisfactorily. That is a good thing to bear in mind—no match is lost before it is played. When a golfer possessed of such ability as had Mr. Herreshoff can be defeated eleven up and nine to play, it simply shows that golf is a game of uncertainties, after all; that, in fact, is one of its great charms.

In that same championship, the uncertainties of the game were shown in another match, and again Mr. Evans was one of the factors, though this time on the losing side. He had been playing in form which made him a distinctive favorite for the title, and, in the semifinal round, he came to the sixteenth hole two up on W. C. Fownes, Jr., of Pittsburgh. The sixteenth is a short hole, just a mashie pitch. Mr. Evans reached the edge of the green with his tee shot, whereas Mr. Fownes made a poor effort, and put his ball in a sand-trap.

Mr. Fownes ran into some trouble on the sixteenth hole when he put his ball in a sand-trap. *(bugphai, courtesy of iStock)*

The match appeared to be over, then and there. But a match in golf never is over until one player has a lead of more holes than there are holes to play, a fact which was demonstrated anew in this match. Mr. Fownes played out of the trap, and holed a long putt for a three, while Mr. Evans, using his mid-iron instead of his putter from the edge of the green, was well past the hole on his second shot, and failed to get the putt coming back. Hence, instead of winning the hole and the match, as he seemed bound to do, he lost the hole. Then, as so often happens when a man apparently has a match absolutely in hand and loses an opening to clinch it, Mr. Evans lost the seventeenth, likewise the home hole, and, with the loss of the eighteenth, he also lost the match. Instead of winning the match and the championship, as nearly everybody figured he would, he only got to the semi-finals. It is true that Mr. Fownes made a wonderful recovery at the sixteenth, to get his three; he played a remarkable shot at the seventeenth, too; but a man is apt to do that after recovering from an almost hopeless situation.

It was in that championship that I was astonished to see such a great golfer as Mr. Evans using his mid-iron instead of his putter most of the time on the greens. He was then following the same practice that was true of his play in the middle west, notwithstanding that the putter is a much superior club for greens such as are found at The Country Club. He could not be expected, of course, to come east and learn to get the best results from the putter in such a short time as he had for practice.

To see him use the mid-iron on the greens, and then practically lose his semifinal round match, and possibly the title, because he could not lay a mid-iron approach-putt dead at the sixteenth, helped me to form one resolution for which I since have been thankful. That was to use my putter from any point on the green, provided there was no special reason for doing otherwise. Of course, there are circumstances when the mid-iron is better for an approach-putt than the putter, as, for example, when there is a little piece of dirt on or in front of the ball, casual water, or uneven surface to go over. But under normal conditions, nowadays, I would rather use my putter and take three putts, than take a mid-iron or another club. By adhering to that policy,

I think I have gained more confidence in my putting, and confidence is a wonderful asset in this branch of the game. Watching the good players in that championship gave me one distinct ambition, which was to try to steady my game down to a point where I would not play four holes well, say, and then have two or three poor ones before getting another three-or four-hole streak of satisfactory play. The steadily good game is better than the combination of brilliant and erratic. It is something like the hare and the tortoise.

CHAPTER 5

BEN HOGAN'S FIRST MAJOR CHAMPIONSHIP

JEFF MILLER

Ben Hogan had one final chance to cap his stellar 1946 season with his first major championship. The P.G.A. Championship would be played in late August at Oregon's Portland Golf Club, the course Hogan had personally annexed during the 1945 Portland Open with the record-sheering 27-under-par 261. Yet Byron Nelson came into the tournament considered at least the cofavorite, despite a sore back, on the basis of being the event's defending champion along with the fact that he'd won three of his last five starts. As Hogan and Nelson reached the quarterfinals, Nelson had little to worry about other than his sacroiliac. He eliminated Frank Rodia 8-and-7 (playing twenty-seven holes in 10-under-par), host pro Larry Lamberger (3-and-2), and his 1943 New York City tour guide, Herman Barron (3-and-2). Hogan's victories to reach the three 18-hole rounds began somewhat tight but became progressively easier. He downed Charles Weisner (2-and-1), Bill Heinlein (4-and-3), and Arthur Bell (5-and-4).

In the quarterfinals that started 36-hole play, Nelson was pitted against "Porky" Oliver while Hogan's foe was Frank Moore. Nelson owned a two-hole lead with five holes to play but couldn't put Oliver away. The match was square going to the thirty-sixth hole, when Nelson yanked his second shot into the woods. That left him needing to convert a 25-foot putt to save par and extend the match beyond regulation; the putt didn't fall, and the

Demaret (left) and Nelson were two tough competitors, but neither managed to beat Hogan in the 1946 P.G.A. Championship. *(AP Photo)*

defending champion was shockingly out in the quarterfinals. There had been talk earlier in the tournament that Nelson was hampered by a bad back, but after being eliminated he denied that. "My back never bothered me at all," Nelson said, sipping a Coke and chewing on some ice. "I lost to a man who shot better golf. Ed's a great guy and a fine competitor."

Meanwhile, the Hogan express continued to pick up steam. He defeated Moore 5-and-4, then routed his pal, Jimmy Demaret, 10-and-9. "Sunny Jim" actually built a lead of 2-up through the match's first three holes, but that only seemed to inject life into Hogan's game. He birdied three of the next four holes to swipe the lead as he completed the morning round 6-up. Afternoon competition wasn't much different. The match was over at twenty-seven holes. The drastic margin of victory prompted reporters to see if the normally jovial Demaret was provoked by Hogan's killer instinct. It was after this round that Demaret contributed to the legion of quotes pertaining to how little Hogan would say while playing. Asked if Hogan talked to him during the one-sided day, Demaret said, "Yes. 'You're away.'"

The final provided a contrast in silhouettes, Hogan at 137 and the somewhat slimmed-down Oliver at about 220. Hogan fell behind by three holes during the morning round because of—naturally—putting predicaments. But he immediately made amends with a 30 on the front nine of his afternoon play, taking a two-hole lead into the back nine. Hogan played the final fourteen holes in 8-under-par and defeated Oliver 6-and-4 to win the Wanamaker Trophy. Henny Bogan had won a major championship. "The only time I was sure of winning was when 'Porky' walked over and shook my hand," Hogan said. "No one gets as many birdies as I did without being lucky, and, boy, was I tickled when those long putts started to drop. It's impossible to explain how much this means to me, so I'll just say, 'Thank you,' to the P.G.A. and my wife, Valerie." The path to a first major championship was so much more of an odyssey, a test of will and skill and guile for Hogan, than it appeared to be for Nelson. Whereas Nelson won the 1937 Masters in only his third season of week-in, week-out Tour competition, Hogan's path covered the better part of eight seasons—which followed the fits and starts that began eight years before that, when he first teed it up as a professional at Brackenridge in San Antonio at the 1930 Texas Open.

Hogan (center) smiles as he receives the PGA Trophy. *(AP Photo/Paul Wagner)*

CHAPTER 6

BREAKING BARRIERS ON THE COURSE

MATTHEW SILVERMAN

Though John Shippen was the first African American to play in the U.S. Open in 1896—and tied for the lead after the first day at Shinnecock Hills, where he was a caddy, before finishing fifth—it took until the 1960s for a black man to regularly play in Professional Golf Association tournaments, a decision that lagged behind the major American sports leagues, as well as tennis.

The other sports had kept African Americans out mostly through an "old boy" network, but the Professional Golfers Association had an article in its bylaws stating that membership was for men of "the Caucasian race." That language was removed in 1961, thanks to African American golfer Lee Spiller, whose long-running suit against the PGA came to the attention of California attorney general Stanley Mosk. He told the PGA it could not use public courses; the PGA replied that it would simply use private courses. When Mosk threatened to start contacting other state attorneys general, the PGA relented.

Charlie Sifford became the first African American on the PGA Tour when he teed up at Sedgefield Country Club at the 1961 Greater Greensboro Open. The golf tee Sifford used might have been the patented invention of the first African American Harvard graduate, George Grant, in 1899, except that the successful Boston dentist never marketed his creation and only gave

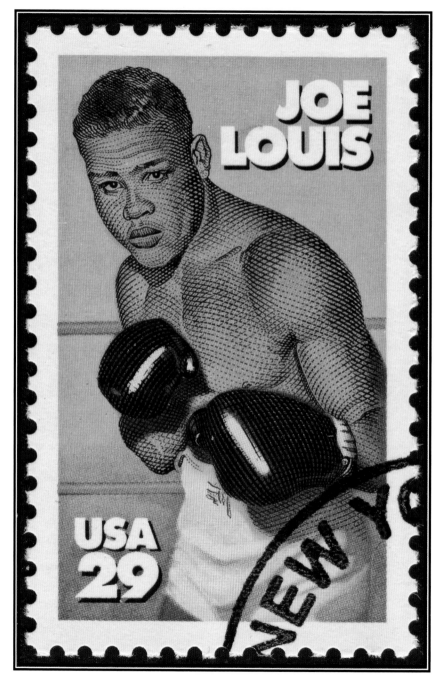

Boxing great Joe Louis was actually the first African American to play in a PGA-sanctioned event. *(traveler1116, courtesy of iStock)*

the tees to friends; a white New Jersey dentist, William Lowell, was the first to mass-produce the idea with the Reddy Tee in the 1920s.

Sifford was thirty-nine years old when he became a PGA rookie, but he was a veteran of the United Golf Association. The UGA had been formed by African American golfers in 1925 in Washington, D.C., six years after Negro League baseball was formed. The goal was to make golf equal for all and to create a means of support, both spiritually and financially. Affectionately known as "The Chitlin' Circuit," Sifford called the UGA "one of the greatest organizations in the world because it gave a lot of people a chance to play golf who didn't have anywhere else to play." Players from all over the country followed the circuit, and everyone wanted a shot at the annual Negro Open, an event Sifford won six times. UGA great Pete Brown recalled that it was called "a picnic" because so many people were on the course; some 200 or 300 would cram onto a course, including whites.

Though Sifford was the first African American to qualify for the PGA Tour, a decade earlier boxing great Joe Louis had been the first black to play in a PGA-sanctioned event—the 1952 San Diego Open. Louis also helped get seven African Americans a qualifying round for the Phoenix Open, a PGA event. Playing in the first foursome with Louis, Brown, and Eural Clark, Sifford recalled in his 1992 book *Just Let Me Play* that he was so excited on the first tee he had to calm himself down after missing the fairway with his drive. He put his second shot on the green, in birdie range, and was about to pull the flagstick when "something seemed funny and I glanced down at the cup. I had the flagstick half raised but I shoved it back into the cup. Somebody had been there before us." The cup was filled with human excrement. Their concentration shattered, none of the men qualified.

Playing on the PGA Tour during the height of the Civil Rights movement, Sifford endured enough threats that he occasionally carried a gun in his golf bag. He won the 1967 Greater Hartford Open and two years later captured the Los Angeles Open in a playoff. Despite his PGA Tour wins and his standing among the top 60 money earners during his first nine years, he was still not invited to play in The Masters.

Tiger Woods has won all four major championships, at least three times each. *(U.S. Navy Petty Officer 2nd Class Molly A. Burgess, courtesy of Wikimedia Commons)*

Lee Elder earned the first trip to The Masters by an African American in 1975. Three years earlier The Masters had gone to the format of including all PGA winners from the previous year, and he was tied for the lead after 72 holes at the 1974 Monsanto Open in Pensacola, Florida, the same course where Elder and other black PGA Tour members had previously been forced to change in the parking lot because the clubhouse was off-limits. Elder won after a four-hole playoff to earn the invite to Augusta—not to mention an escort in a police car from the Pensacola Country Club clubhouse because of death threats.

Elder didn't make the cut at the 1975 Masters, but he heard cheers throughout his two rounds. He played there four times but the closest he came to winning was a tie for 17th in 1979. In 1997 Elder was in such a hurry to get to Augusta as a spectator that he received a speeding ticket. He did not want to miss Tiger Woods dominating the course. His 12-stroke victory lap at Augusta in 1997 was the first time an African American had won a golf major. Woods has since won the other three majors . . . at least three times apiece.

Though the "Tiger Woods craze" was good for golf, there has been no influx of young African American players joining the Tour who would have grown up idolizing Woods. Part of the reasoning, some think, is that the golf cart has replaced the caddie at all but a few select country clubs. Watching others play golf and being around the course has created some of the greatest players in the last century, of all races.

Programs like The First Tee have provided young people and minorities with chances to play golf that they probably would not have had, reaching some five million participants since its inception in 1997. The pro ranks may not yet be filled with The First Tee graduates, but progress in the wake of the dramatic steps taken by Elders and Siffords and even Shippens may take time. Just creating more people who love the game, whether their aspirations are to turn pro or just break 90, is another step forward.

CHAPTER 7

MY EARLY DAYS ON THE LINKS

CECIL LEITCH

J UST beyond Silloth, on the left side of the road that leads to the pretty little village of Skinburness (once a flourishing market town which was washed away by a terrific storm), there used to be a stretch of natural seaside ground remembered by Sillothians as "The Banks"—"used to be," for gradually the encroaching waters of Solway Firth have eaten it away, until little remains of the bonnie "Banks" of my childhood.

Although I love the dear old Solway in all its moods, I can never forgive it for this act of destruction. In devouring "The Banks" it destroyed the actual birthplace of my golf, the spot where I first hit a golf ball, disregarding the sanctity that always attaches to a birthplace. For that, it can never be forgiven.

It was here on this strip of land, about 200 yards wide and stretching away into the distance, intersected by numerous paths made by those who took their daily walks overlooking the Solway Firth, that I, at the age of about nine, in company with my elder sister May, began my golfing career.

Had my family or I known at that time that I should one day be called upon to perpetrate a golfing autobiography, a careful record would, no doubt, have been kept of the year, the day, and the hour when I first struck a golf ball and of all later developments.

Happily we did not know, and memory, though not such an accurate recorder as written memoranda, must be relied upon for the earlier dates and facts.

Going back to my extreme infancy, to the days beyond the reach of my memory, I was, my elders tell me, just the everyday child, with, however, one unusual predilection for a girl: I preferred whips to dolls. Dolls held no attraction for me—my heart's affections ran to whips—and at the mature age of two and a half I insisted on being photographed with a whip in my hands. The imaginative will, of course, see in this the germ of the future golfer!

Between this and the beginnings of my golf, that is between the ages of two and nine, I spent most of my time on the seashore at Silloth, my native place. My father was a Scotsman, a doctor by profession, and my mother English, so that I am an Anglo-Scot. Living in England, we had only to look a few miles across the water to see Scotland, a happy blend which seemed to express our Anglo-Scottish descent.

Silloth lies in a remote northwest corner of England, on the coast of Cumberland, 20 miles from Carlisle, the capital of the county, and 320 miles

Leitch was born in Silloth, England. *(Humphrey Bolton, from geograph.org.uk; courtesy of Wikimedia Commons)*

from London. Its residential population is under three thousand, but in the summer it is crowded with visitors, for as a seaside resort Silloth is very popular in the North of England. Fishing, a harbour, and a flour mill represent the industrial activities of the place, with the agriculture, which is the chief interest of the district. From Silloth, the coast of Scotland can always be seen, while on super-bright days the Isle of Man, 60 miles away, is clearly visible. But this latter is an evil omen, greatly feared by golfers; for it augurs rain, much rain, within three days. Quite apart from the natural affection one has for one's birthplace, Silloth is a lovable place, and casts its pleasant spell especially on those who haunt the links. Golfing visitors feel this and return again and again.

My father was the pioneer of golf at Silloth, laying out a nine-hole course on common land and playing there, with his sister, the first game of golf ever played on the shores of the Solway Firth. The natives of the place regarded them as a pair of lunatics. So there were hereditary reasons why I should not only play golf, but become "mad" on the game. And I may say here that never once since I first took a club in my hand has there been any doubt about my love for golf; my love for it has never faltered; neither victory nor defeat has made any difference; I have just gone on growing fonder and fonder of the game, and nothing in the whole of my golfing career has been harder to bear than my banishment from the links after returning from America, the result of an injured arm.

At the age of nine then, I began my golfing career, on a stretch of ground 200 yards wide and a quarter of a mile long; for this was all we made use of for our primitive nine-hole course. Our fairways were the paths made by pedestrians, our putting greens the good patches on these paths, our holes cut by ourselves and lined with treacle tins, and our "trouble" the bents, sand holes, and wiry grass common to seaside links.

My first club was one of the old-fashioned cleeks, and my first ball— and only one for a long time—a guttie. This was my introduction to the game, and in its independence, it bears a close relationship to the rest of my golfing career. My golf has developed along independent lines; I am entirely self-taught, and I never had a lesson in my life. I watched others of course, and learnt from them, avoiding their faults and, no doubt, assimilating some of the good features of their play. Then I have received many valuable tips from leading players—from Mr. Hilton, who impressed upon me the importance of firmly gripping the ground with my feet; from the late Tom Ball, who taught me a cut shot with an iron; from Arnaud Massy, from whom I learnt an effective approach shot, and from several others, while I know no better corrective for "off one's game" than having a round with a first-class amateur or professional. Watching his even, rhythmical swing, one soon finds oneself falling into his way of doing it. It is a sort of unconscious mimicry.

But though I certainly owe a good deal to others, I am essentially a self-taught golfer. This should encourage, rather than discourage young players.

I think we must have played for about three years on our little makeshift course before joining the Carlisle and Silloth Golf Club. My brother Monie (the family consisted of five girls and two boys) and my sister Edith were already members of the Club, and the former had begun to show himself a player of much promise.

When I say that the ladies' annual subscription at that time was only five shillings, it will be seen that my sisters and I were not very important assets so far as the Club's income was concerned. Nor did we seem to be important in other respects. Ladies and children were a rare sight on the links, and no one appeared to take much notice of us, or to be troubled by our existence.

I well remember that my sister May and I (we usually played together) were too timid to drive off from the first tee, which is in full view of the Clubhouse, for some time after we had every right to do so.

By this time I had been promoted to a bag, and from one club to a set of six, as follows: driver, the favorite and veteran cleek, lofting iron, mashie, niblick and putter.

My sister May, a left-handed player, had begun her golf with a cleek, a club with which she has always been an adept. Great difficulty was experienced in persuading the professional, at that time, to make a left-handed club for a child. He argued that she ought to be made to play in the ordinary right-handed way.

May is undoubtedly left-handed and always has been; she plays tennis with the left hand, and invariably uses the left hand when other people would use the right. Many children want to play in a left-handed manner, but few are actually left-handed. The professional, no doubt, had it in his mind that May was one of these. However, he made her her left-handed clubs and, judging from the way she used them, with just as much care as if they had been right-handed.

It must have been during this very raw stage of our apprenticeship that a male member of the Club witnessed the following incident, which he long after related to us. "I was playing golf at Silloth" (to give it in his own words) "one day many years ago, and, arriving at the 14th, or Heather hole, my partner and I came across two little curly-haired girls dressed alike in white sailor coats, blue serge kilted skirts, white socks and little black patent-leather ankle-strap slippers. One was hacking away in the heather, while the other stood with her legs crossed and looked on. After many fruitless efforts by the smaller to dislodge the ball, she turned round and, in a pathetic voice exclaimed, 'I can't get it out!' To which the other answered, 'No, it needs strength and you lack it.'" This little story certainly has the ring of truth, for Silloth heather is plentiful and thick, terrible stuff to escape from. I paid it frequent visits and also I was not nearly as strong as my sister May.

And here let me say that this constant playing on a course where heather and sand, bents and wind abounded was the best possible education for the young golfer with any grit or gift for the game. The trying conditions might have discouraged some, but never did us. We loved the buffetings of the wind and the high adventure of the difficulties, and these things gave a fibre to our game which easier conditions would never have given. Wind was almost the normal condition at Silloth, and one's game had to be adapted accordingly. Experience teaches the best and most permanent lessons, and even in the earlier and more irresponsible days Silloth was teaching me lessons which have left their mark on my game. Constant battling with the wind gradually evolved in me a means of reducing its resistance, and much familiarity with difficult "lies" on or off the course bred in me, if not exactly a contempt for them, at any rate no great fear of them.

We never allowed either wind or weather to curtail a round once started. We persevered until our balls were at the bottom of the last hole, determined to see the thing through. I am sure this was good for us and developed in us the spirit of fighting to a finish when it came to important match play.

No sooner had I joined the Carlisle and Silloth Club than I began to keep a record of every round or match played. To this day I have kept up that practice.

Had circumstances allowed, we would have played golf every day and all day; but education and its claims forbade this. There is no doubt that education does interfere with a child's golf! I am not sure that it is not a greater nuisance in that way than work in later life!

Everyone knows the story of the ardent golfer who told a friend that golf was interfering with business, and that he would have to give it up. "What!" exclaimed his friend, "give up golf?" "No," replied the other, "business." That was my feeling about golf and education.

As a matter of fact we had little to grumble at. After being started off in our education at home, we went to school in Carlisle for many years. This necessitated an hour's train journey morning and afternoon; but as we got back to Silloth by three o'clock on most days, we had time for a round of golf nearly every day during the summer months. The guard of the train, Mr. Selkirk, an official well known to visitors and golfers, often speaks of the responsibility he felt in looking after the four of us. I think it says a great deal for our sense of duty that we never once missed the train. To have done so would, probably, have meant a day's golf! The temptation was great, and it would have been such a simple matter to succumb to it. A little lagging or imaginary trouble with a boot-lace was all that was necessary. But I must not take all the credit to ourselves for our regular attendance at school. Our friend, the guard, was largely responsible for it. Many were the times he stood at the end of the platform, whistle and flag in hand, beckoning to one, two, three, or even four small figures trailing stationwards. That particular train had not a good reputation for punctuality. It was a very different story coming back; there was only eagerness to get to the station as soon as possible.

Arrived at Silloth, we invariably made for the Clubhouse and, throwing our school-bags into the locker and our school worries with them, set off from the first tee full of hope that we should play the game of our life.

Not long after its publication, I became the proud possessor of a copy of Braid's book, *Advanced Golf*. How I used to devour this in the train to and from school. Alas! my zeal for the study of Braid outran my discretion. One day, under cover of the lid of my desk, I was secretly feeding on Braid when my mental diet should have been of a more edifying (!) kind. Detection was followed by confiscation, and *Advanced Golf* spent several unhappy and profitless days in the mistress's desk.

Leitch took a strong interest in *Advanced Golf*, written by James Braid. *(Ronnie Leask, from geograph.org.uk; courtesy of Wikimedia Commons)*

Our keenness for golf was not at all understood by the schoolmistresses. On returning to school after the summer holidays, we were, on one occasion, told to write an essay on how we had spent them. We, of course, had spent ours on the links; but the innocent colloquial golfing expression, "Spent my holidays on the links," was taken as a gross exaggeration by the mistress and underlined as such.

One of the questions in a geography examination paper was: "What do you know about the denudation of the earth's surface ?" Having no idea what "denudation" meant, I had, perforce, to give this question a miss. But when later I learnt the meaning of denudation, and its geological significance, I felt I had let slip the chance of a lifetime, for my own practical experience of denudation on the Silloth links fitted me to write feelingly on the subject.

I had my favourite subjects at school and worked hard enough at these, which, perhaps fittingly, were mathematics, science, drawing, and physical geography, especially those parts of the last named dealing with the composition of the earth's surface and with climatic conditions. Political geography made no appeal to me. It might have been otherwise had I known that the game I loved would one day take me to many different parts of the world. Though school prizes never fell to my share, I had the satisfaction of always being in a class where I was younger than the average age.

At home we were always encouraged in outdoor games, our mother maintaining that it was far better for our health to forget lessons entirely on leaving school each day. Nor did she believe in too much home-work. For these beliefs we blessed her! Hockey, cricket, and tennis were included in the school curriculum, but, though keen on these, I would willingly have given them all up for golf.

The energy of a child, viewed through adult eyes, is an amazing thing. Many times, in those early days, did I play three rounds of the Silloth course in one day. Remembering the number of shots and the amount of energy I used to expend per round, I wonder I was not often exhausted. And yet I do not recollect ever feeling even tired. But the bracing air of Silloth must share the credit for this. Limpness is a feeling I, personally, have never experienced at Silloth, though I have played on courses where I hardly had the energy to drag one foot after the other.

In another respect, too, I was very fortunate in having Silloth for my native course. A large-minded and generous Committee allowed children the full privileges of the links. What a blessing this was has often been forcibly brought to my mind when hearing of boys and girls unable to play over their local courses, and unable, therefore, to make an early start at the game.

As I knocked a guttie ball round the Silloth links by the means I found most comfortable, I had no prophetic vision that golf would be the cause of my travelling thousands of miles, playing before thousands of spectators, making multitudes of friends, experiencing countless thrills and excitements, and achieving success in the great big golfing world. I understood as a child, I thought as a child, I played as a child.

Soon after joining the Club, I was taking part in Club matches and competitions. A Leitch usually headed the latter, while in the former the Leitch family furnished the majority of the team. An amusing incident of one of these matches is worth retelling. The Silloth team, largely Leitch in flavour, journeyed to Moffat to play the local Club. After mutual greetings, the Moffat captain, seeing two small children with the team, remarked to the Silloth captain, "Oh, you needn't have brought caddies with you, we have plenty here." Her embarrassment on learning that the "caddies" were members of the team was only second to her amazement when later the little sisters returned to the Club-house, bringing with them the scalps of their adult opponents.

During all this time we were quite unconscious of the fact that we played any better than other ordinary mortals in the outside world. And it was not until Mr. Eustace White, the well-known writer on women's sport, paid a chance visit to Silloth in 1907, that we were led to believe we were anything more than beginners.

The great names in ladies' golf were known to us, and we read with keen interest of the doings of Rhona Adair, Lottie Dod and the Hezlets. But they were just names to us, golfing goddesses, too far above us to make us either envious or ambitious. A story I was told about Rhona Adair impressed me.

She was playing on a course laid out over rocky ground. Before using a spoon for which she had great affection, she would pull a hatpin from her hat and test the ground with it, in case a hidden rock should damage her pet club.

When not playing myself, I loved nothing so much as "carrying" for my brother, especially when he was taking part in a Club match or competition. He used very few clubs: brassie, driving iron, jigger, mashie and putter. He would never have these cleaned and became known as the boy with the "bronze set of clubs." Though he was not exceptionally long, his short game was the most marvellous thing imaginable. I have yet to see its equal. He never had a handicap worse than scratch, and on winning with ease the first competition he took part in as a full member, he was made plus 2, a handicap he retained till his early death in 1907, at the age of twenty-two.

We all learned our golf with the old guttie ball, and I am glad of it. That old solid ball had to be hit in the proper manner before it would go. There was no running bunkers with it, and a "top" meant an ugly gash that made one realize the fault must not be repeated. One great advantage it had over the rubber-cored ball was that it could be re-made. Often on hitting one hard on the head, I found consolation in the fact that it was a 27 1/2 and that Renouf, who was the professional at the time, would give me a re-made for it, together with sixpence. I never remember experiencing the drudgery stage, through which most players have to pass. All being self-taught, our styles were quite different. Of the sisters, Edith, the eldest, was always looked up to by the others, as she was, undoubtedly, the most capable performer. My allotted place was No. 3. The wind and the guttie ball together had an influence on our style, and produced in us our powerful and rather manlike swings.

Since success has come my way, two or three professionals claim to have taught me my golf. But surely no professional would allow a pupil to adopt, to the extent to which I do, the palm grip, flat swing, and bent knee at the top of the swing. Such an unorthodox combination should be condemned and disowned by the professional teacher!

There is a famous hole at Silloth called the "Duffer's Bunker." A very wide and deep sand pit has to be carried from the tee. This used to be the dread of lady (and many men) players, especially in a medal round, as it came near the end (formerly the 16th, now the 17th). To this day I can remember the exquisite thrill of pleasure at my first successful "crack" over this trouble.

The improvement in my play came gradually, and I was encouraged by friends interested in my efforts to keep on improving my "best round." The day I broke 100 by one stroke was a red-letter day. Slowly and surely I improved this, until at the age of seventeen (the year of my first championship), my average match-play round was between 80 and 84 from the men's tees, bogey at that time being about 78.

In the summer of 1907 Mrs. Archbold Smith, a moving spirit in Yorkshire golf, paid a golfing visit to Silloth. She tried hard to make us believe that we played better than most of the competitors in the ladies' open championship. But we did not share this flattering opinion of our own play, and would certainly have gasped had anyone predicted that one of us would come within measurable distance of winning the open championship in less than a year.

CHAPTER 8

THE JOPLIN GHOST

DAVID BARRETT

It was disappointing that Bobby Jones wasn't in real contention after 36 holes, but the tournament was led by a man who at one time was supposed to be the next Bobby Jones.

Horton Smith burst out of Missouri at the age of twenty in 1928–29 with such force that he still stands as the most accomplished player at an early age the PGA Tour has ever seen—including Tiger Woods. Here are the all-time Tour leaders in victories before a given age:

21st birthday—Horton Smith 8, Gene Sarazen 3, Tiger Woods 2
22nd birthday—Horton Smith 12, Tiger Woods 6, Gene Sarazen 4
23rd birthday—Horton Smith 14, Tiger Woods 7, Gene Sarazen 4
24th birthday—Horton Smith 15, Tiger Woods 15, Jack Nicklaus 8
25th birthday—Tiger Woods 23, Horton Smith 17, Jack Nicklaus 12

Smith was twenty-five at the time of the 1934 Masters. While he was playing too well to be called washed up, he was yesterday's news. While his good friend Paul Runyan had stepped into the spotlight, Smith had slipped into the shadows. Now in a tournament featuring the return to competition of Bobby Jones, Smith was staging a comeback of his own—from relative mediocrity.

Smith had won only one tournament in the previous seventeen months, and that was with Runyan as his partner at the 1933 Miami International Four-Ball. The perception was that Runyan had done most of the heavy

Horton Smith, pictured here with his caddy, was yesterday's news by the time of the 1934 Masters. *(Courtesy of the Boston Public Library, Leslie Jones Collection)*

lifting there and carried Smith to victory. In a poll of forty-two PGA players taken in November 1933, not a single one voted for Smith as one of the top ten players.

When he was taking the tour by storm five years earlier, Smith was called the "Joplin Ghost" because he was based out of Joplin, Missouri, and he was exceedingly hard to catch once he had the lead. For much of the period 1931 to 1933 he was a ghost in the sense that his presence was barely felt.

Smith actually hailed from Springfield, Missouri, not Joplin. He spent his early years on a small farm seven miles outside of town before his family made the fortuitous move to a 31-acre farm directly across from Springfield Country Club.

His father, Perry, made his living primarily by buying and selling cattle, so what farming was done on their place was done by Horton, his older brother Ren, and his mother. As a result, Horton was hardened by farm labor but also had the advantages of being from a relatively prosperous family due to the success of his father's business.

One of those advantages was joining the country club. His father didn't play much golf, but got a family membership after Horton and Ren got into the game as caddies. Not that Springfield was an elite club with impeccably manicured fairways. In fact, Smith said that it wasn't until he started playing on the tour that he realized the fairways of a golf course ought to have playable lies. "This makes a great deal of difference," he told a reporter.

Springfield had sand greens, but Smith nonetheless became one of the best putters of his time. He said that learning the game on sand greens actually helped him, because being able to see the track of the ball not only enabled him to get a feel for the line of the putt but also to develop a level stroke—if he hit up on the ball too much, he could see how the ball skipped at the start instead of rolling; if he hit down on it, he could see where the blade of his putter contacted the sand.

The club's professional, Neal Cross, took Smith under his wing. When Horton was fifteen, Cross arranged for Horton to caddie for Walter Hagen in an exhibition match, and that same year Smith won the club and city championships. At sixteen, he was a semifinalist in the Western Junior. A bright kid and a good student, Smith matriculated at State Teachers College in Springfield. But he really wanted to apply his mind to what really fascinated him—the game of golf. What's more, he wanted to make it his profession, and felt that he had the ability to be successful at it.

"He saw in it the possibilities of a business career, just as others see the same promise in law, medicine, and finance," Joe Williams would write in the *New York Telegram* less than four years later, when Smith had already made it big.

Given the small monetary rewards in golf compared to those other professions, it was a vision that was hard for others to see, including Horton's father, who said, "But there's no future, no money, nothing in golf."

"It will have a future if I am any good at it," Horton replied.

"Well, son, do whatever you like, but convince me as soon as you can that there is a future in it," said his dad.

Just before his eighteenth birthday in May 1926, Smith became an assistant pro and caddie master at Springfield Country Club and later that year showed his notion of making a living as a player was not a pipedream when he finished tenth in the Heart of America Open, a tour event in St. Louis. The next year he worked simultaneously at clubs in three Missouri towns on different days of the week and also qualified for the 1927 U.S. Open, making the cut at Oakmont less than a month after turning nineteen.

His ambition fired, Smith was able to get a Springfield man named A. H. Hill to advance him $1,000 so he could play the western and southwestern portions of the winter tour of 1927–28, telling him he felt he could make decent money on the circuit if he had some decent clothes, a good set of clubs, and enough cash so he wouldn't have to worry about getting home. "My dad could have let me have that money, but I would have felt like I was under pressure all the time if I was using his money to play," Smith said later. "But Mr. Hill had it and wanted to loan it."

Smith played in fourteen tournaments, finishing in the money in all but one. He broke even financially, while gaining valuable experience.

He parlayed that success to a better club job at Oak Hill Country Club in Joplin in 1928, with his older brother as his assistant. But the Joplin Ghost would only stay in Joplin for one season—by the next year his life had become a whirlwind of tournaments, exhibition matches, and public acclaim.

It all started in September in Kansas City, where the young pro made the field for the PGA Championship despite carding an eight and a nine on the second and fourth holes of the 36-hole qualifying. Still deep in the trees after six strokes on the fourth hole, Smith stooped down to pick up his ball and withdraw.

"All of a sudden I realized I was quitting," he later recalled. "I straightened up, grabbed a club, hit the ball out, made a nine with one putt, and kept going. That day made me. It taught me perseverance and to never give up and was a helpful thing the rest of my life. I've never forgotten that day. It changed my whole career."

Smith qualified with scores of 79–70—149 despite a 44 on his first nine holes. Then in the PGA Championship at Baltimore Country Club he made it to the semifinals. He was on his way.

Smith's first victory came a month later in November 1928 at the Oklahoma City Open. After losing a two-stroke lead on the first hole of the final round, Smith's lesson in perseverance paid off. He not only kept his cool, he hit a perfect shot on the par-three second hole and made a hole-in-one to take the lead for good.

"First prize was a thousand dollars," Smith recalled. "It seemed like a million to me."

Horton Smith beat out Walter Hagen (pictured here), the best professional at the time, in a nine-hole tournament in 1928. *(Courtesy of the Boston Public Library, Leslie Jones Collection)*

Smith claimed his second win on Christmas Eve at the Santa Catalina Island Open in California. The tournament was held on a little nine-hole, par-32 course, but it was significant nonetheless because Smith outdueled Hagen, the game's glamour boy and best professional. Smith's scores of 63–58–61–63 gave him an 11-under 245 total, one ahead of Hagen and 11 strokes clear of third place as the two were the class of the field.

Hagen was so impressed with that showing and another Smith win at the Pensacola Open in early 1929 that he named the twenty-year-old to the United States Ryder Cup team that would compete in England in April. Since steel shafts were still outlawed in Great Britain (they wouldn't be legalized there until 1930), Smith decided to acclimatize himself to hickory shafts at the Belleair Open, which resulted in him finishing out of the money.

Going back to steel, Smith turned into a juggernaut, winning his next four individual tournaments. He beat Denny Shute in a playoff at the Fort Myers Open, where the two of them played 47 holes the final day—the last two regulation rounds, a scheduled nine-hole playoff that ended in a tie, and a hastily arranged agreement to play sudden death (a rare format for that era), which Smith won on the second hole.

After losing with partner Al Watrous in the match-play International Four-Ball, Smith captured the Florida Open in Jacksonville before heading to the richest event on the tour that year, Miami's La Gorce Open. Smith claimed the enormous first prize of $5,000 plus a $1,000 gold plate with a two-stroke victory over Ed Dudley.

Back home his father, who usually haunted the Associated Press room of the Springfield News and Leader on the final day of tournaments, stayed away this time. "I was afraid," he later told the paper. Horton was able to send the big winner's check to his father as proof that there was a future in golf—and that it hadn't taken long for him to show it.

Smith beat a field at La Gorce that included Hagen, Sarazen, reigning U.S. Open champion Johnny Farrell, Tommy Armour, Bill Mehlhorn, and virtually everybody who was anybody in golf, except, of course, for amateur Bobby Jones, the greatest player of them all.

Smith's spectacular run was earning him comparisons with Jones, and who better to make that evaluation than O. B. Keeler, Jones's chronicler and traveling companion? Keeler covered the tour's next event, the North and South Open in Pinehurst, North Carolina, and this is what he observed.

"[Smith is] cool, composed, as modest as a kid popularly is supposed to be and usually isn't, the best-looking youngster I have laid my eyes on since Bobby Jones was a boy wonder, and I can't say if he looks better than Bobby did at that age because they are radically different in all parts of style.

"Where Bobby is short and stocky, Horton Smith is tall and lanky. Where the Jones shoulders are broad and his chest is thick, the Smith shoulders are sloping. Curiously enough, the Smith swing is shorter than the Jones swing; Horton is just between a full and a three-quarters swing in the big shots, leisurely going back and coming through with a magnificent lashing impact. But where they do agree is a vital point—a perfectly straight left arm through all the shots until well after impact."

Smith shot a 67 in the morning round of the 36-hole final day at the North and South to propel him to a two-stroke victory over 1927 U.S. Open champion Armour. It gave him seven wins, along with three runner-up finishes, in eighteen tournaments on the five-month winter tour.

"He is a greater golfer than I expected to see and I expected to see a very great one," Keeler concluded.

With word circulating at Pinehurst that Jones was considering retiring, "The question of the Atlantan's successor naturally arose," wrote United Press sports editor Frank Getty. "At the moment it looks as if Horton Smith, at twenty, stood the best chance of filling Bobby's shoes as the outstanding golfer in the world."

Hagen wasn't so sure. Asked by a gallery member at the International Four-Ball how Smith compared with Jones, the Haig responded, "There's only one Jones. We'll never see another like him—at least we'll not live to see him."

Nonetheless, Hagen was very impressed by Smith, saying, "He's got every shot in the bag."

There was another thing that noted raconteur Hagen observed about the kid from Missouri. "He doesn't smoke, drink, or give a rap about girls," Hagen said. "I have yet to hear about the boy or girl who can keep him out after nine o'clock."

Asked whether Smith was missing out on a lot of fun by not mingling with "the boys," Hagen joked, "A helluva lot; he doesn't know he's alive," before adding, "But that is his business and I'm proud of him for it."

Indeed, Smith came across as a straight-laced country boy from America's heartland: modest and amiable, not displaying much of a personality or sense of humor but taking everything in with a pleasant grin and not letting much bother him.

"Despite his youth, he possesses the poise of a veteran," wrote John D. Nash in the New York Post. "All this adulation and gallery worship is new to him, but he accepts it gracefully, and always with that broad, infectious smile that has endeared him to thousands on his junket across the country. It must seem quite strange to this big country boy to have throngs clamoring at his heels, seeking his autograph, a scrap of paper he might let fall, a little tee— anything . . . that the lad possessed, to carry home as a souvenir.

"With each new conquest his popularity increases. Large galleries often serve to unsettle the most hardened vet, but Smith seems to blend perfectly with the crowd. If he is jostled, there is a smile for the culprit. Everyone calls him Horton, and with that rustic characteristic for familiarity, he seems to relish it."

Warren Brown of the *Chicago Herald and Examiner* wrote that Smith "is an easygoing youngster who refuses to let his golf bother him greatly, if at all. In temperament he is in some respects not unlike Walter Hagen. I have yet to hear Hagen explain what would have happened to his score if such and such had or hadn't taken place. Smith is like that. If he hits a bad shot, he doesn't let it dismay him. There is always another shot coming along.

"Smith has no conceit whatever. He is an extremely likeable youngster, always wearing a grin, as if he wonders what the fuss is all about."

Back home in Springfield, family friend Dr. Wilbur Smith said of Horton, "In all the years I've known him, I've never seen him hit the turf or use a profane word." The secrets to his success, Dr. Smith said, were "clean living, clean thinking, hard work, and an even disposition."

Another key to Horton's success was that he was a keen student of the game. He credited his improvement from his first winter tour to his domination in his second year to being able to observe the swings of other pros and talking to them about their technique. Later in 1929 when he made his first trip to Europe, he made sure to talk to past-his-prime British great Harry Vardon about the golf swing.

While learning from others, Smith developed an idiosyncratic technique that best suited his six-foot-one frame and the new steel shafts.

"There was very little question of the full, free-flowing type of swing [of which Jones was the prime example] being the ideal," Smith later wrote. "It didn't work for me though, and probably not for others of my type of build. I retained the essentials of my predecessors but worked out a relatively short swing which began giving me excellent results during the tournaments in 1929."

Indeed, Smith's backswing was the shortest of any of the top pros of the day. He wasn't one of the longer hitters (nor was he among the shortest), but he was very accurate. Hagen, who tended to be wild off the tee, admired Smith's "devilish straightness."

Hagen also said that Smith was Jones's equal on chip shots around the green. But it was on the putting surfaces that Horton stood out.

"Horton was the best putter I've ever seen," said Runyan, who himself had a deserved reputation as a great putter. "To mention anyone else in the same breath is a travesty. He planted himself parallel to the intended line and was sound technically. But what made him a great putter was his attitude. He had a dogged determination to do it the same way, week after week and year after year. Unlike everyone else, he never changed putters unless he was playing well. As he explained it to me, when he did change, he wasn't hoping. He was doing it with considered judgment. Then if he went back to the old putter, he did so with more confidence."

Runyan was on the mark about Smith's devotion to a single method. Associated Press writer Paul Mickelson made the mistake in 1934 of asking Smith if he had a new system of putting.

"No. When you get a sound system—a sound system I said—don't change it. Develop it," Smith replied. "That's the problem with a lot of excellent golfers. They get a sound putting touch, then they get a bad round and start experimenting. As a result, they get a hodgepodge system that ruins their game."

Smith was ahead of his time in giving a lot of thought to the psychology of the game. "What makes a man a champion in golf is the capacity for cooling and quieting the nerves at the right time," he wrote in a magazine article. "There are so many great players who are practically equal in the execution of all shots that we have to look to something besides technical ability to explain successful scoring performances.

"Each championship is two championships; one the championship that I play so people can see it and the other, the one that I have to play inside myself. If I can retain within myself a mental advantage over the rest of the field, I then can benefit from the confidence that shot for shot on the practice tee or green, I am as good as any of them."

Golf was seldom far from Horton's mind. When the members of the Ryder Cup team gathered for some sightseeing in New York before boarding a ship to England, Smith was having the sights pointed out to him from the roof of the New York Athletic Club when he was distracted by a niblick with a very large head that one of the party had with him. He immediately grabbed it and started hitting imaginary shots. "Have you ever seen a niblick like this?" he asked.

Smith was one of only two Americans to win his singles match at the Ryder Cup as the United States fell to Great Britain, but that was just the start of an extended stay in Europe. The British Open followed in early May, and Grantland Rice was sure that Smith could overcome the "hoodoo" that seemed to affect American stars from Walter Travis to John McDermott to Francis Ouimet to Walter Hagen and even Bobby Jones in their first British Open. "He has worked his way to an almost flawless swing. No man in golf hits the ball truer or better with every club," Rice wrote. "He also has a wise, cool head and a stout heart."

Alas, Smith succumbed to the weather—or the hoodoo—and finished twenty-first as Hagen took the claret jug. But moving across the English Channel to the French Open, Smith showed that the hype was justified. Nobody could remember a better one-day display of golf than his 66–66 in the first two rounds at St. Cloud Country Club in Paris, which gave him a twelve-stroke lead. "I've seen only two or three other persons to compare with him," said British pro George Duncan, who played with Smith. "Harry Vardon, Bobby Jones, and Walter Hagen."

The next day he strode to a comfortable victory and was greeted on the 18th green by Hagen holding a birthday cake, for Smith turned twenty-one that day. That evening he attended a party, where he was introduced to one of the guests, a young woman.

"Will you have a cigarette?" she offered.

"I don't smoke," he said.

"How about a drink?" she asked.

"Thanks, but I don't drink," he replied.

"Don't you have any bad habits?" she persisted.

"Yes, I'm short with too many putts."

Smith continued on to Germany, finishing second in the German Open before returning to the States. All eyes were on him at the U.S. Open, where he finally would compete in the same tournament as Jones. That proved to be a disappointment, as Smith finished in a tie for tenth, eight strokes behind Jones, who defeated Al Espinosa in a playoff.

There would be no need for Smith to return to his club job in Joplin. He had become enough of a celebrity that he was booked for a hundred exhibitions with Hagen. Eleven of those came on consecutive days leading up to the U.S. Open, leaving them with only two practice rounds—probably not the best preparation. The rest were packed into July through October, including one period of thirty-three consecutive days—and one event in Boston where they pitted their best ball against an archer shooting arrows from tee to green.

Though their personalities could hardly have been more different, and Hagen was fifteen years older, the two nonetheless hit if off and became good friends. Smith said of Hagen, "He enjoyed fancy clothes, a little drink, and the ladies, but it would have been absolutely impossible for him to have been a complete playboy and still maintain the physical and mental endurance required to play championship golf. Stories of his heavy drinking were exaggerated or false. He had a host of friends and enjoyed many parties with them. And he always had a drink in his hand. But one or two drinks would last a whole evening."

Stories of Hagen being late to the first tee weren't exaggerated, however. He was such a gate attraction—and a charmer—that he could get away with showing up late to tournaments (except for the U.S. and British Opens and the PGA Championship, where he was sure to be on time). Smith said Hagen didn't do it for the purposes of intimidation or to gain attention.

"He was just the slowest individual I ever saw," said Smith, who at first was frustrated when Hagen was late for exhibitions but grew to accept it. "One day when Walter was shaving, I realized that we would be late. I urged him to hurry. He did nothing but smile and never hurried at all. Finally, he told me that if he expected to have a fine, smooth, unhurried stroke on the golf course that day, he did not think the proper method of getting himself into the tempo for the day would be by rushing his razor blade."

Hagen didn't play a full tournament schedule, but Smith went straight from his exhibition tour to nonstop travel on the winter tour. That earned him a new nickname: the Missouri Rover.

Smith won three times before the calendar turned, giving him a total of eight wins and $15,000 in earnings in 1929. Two more wins in the first three months of 1930 gave him five wins on the 1929–30 winter tour—not quite the haul of the previous winter but still impressive.

Along the way, he became the first pro to use a sand wedge and the last to beat Jones before the great amateur retired. Smith learned about the sand wedge in February 1930 from an acquaintance in Houston who introduced him to E. K. McClain, a cotton broker and average golfer who had invented a new kind of niblick designed to get the ball out of the bunker. It had a large, concave face and was very heavy, weighing twenty-three ounces.

Bobby Jones (pictured here in 1932) described his friendship with Horton Smith in his book *Golf is My Game*. *(Courtesy of the Boston Public Library, Leslie Jones Collection)*

McClain wanted to see if he could get one of the major manufacturers to make the club, and Smith, having recently signed with Hagen's new equipment company, said he would take a look at it. After getting good results with it, Smith convinced the company to manufacture the club.

The first tournament where Smith used the sand wedge was the Savannah Open, which was also a noteworthy event because of a memorable duel with Jones, who was using this event and another one in Augusta the following month as tune-ups for his bid at the Grand Slam. A mutual acquaintance arranged for Smith and Jones to room together in Savannah.

"It was the beginning of a long and close friendship, which has been a rich experience for me," Jones later wrote in *Golf Is My Game*. "Both on and off the golf course, Horton has always been a model of his profession and a credit to golf.

"Of course, we two roommates had a very good time together. I think we both liked one another from the beginning, and we had a lot of fun talking golf, practicing swings, and exchanging pointers in the room and going to movies in the evening after dinner."

The tournament became a game of "Can you top this?" between them. Jones set a course record of 67 in the first round, Smith established a new mark with a 66 in the second, and Jones came right back with a 65 in the third. The two were tied at 207 entering the final round. No course records were set in the final round, but Smith, knowing that Jones had completed play with a 279 total, parred his way home on the closing holes for a one-stroke victory. These two great players left the rest of the field far behind, with Jones six strokes ahead of third place.

Smith wasn't scheduled to play in the Southeastern Open in Augusta, but organizers were desperate to promote another duel between Smith and Jones. Smith was playing in the North and South Open in North Carolina on Tuesday and Wednesday (36 holes each day), and he was booked for exhibitions on Thursday and Friday in Charlotte and Asheville and then a golf-show appearance in Boston on Monday. The Southeastern Open was scheduled for Friday, Saturday, and Sunday.

Augusta Country Club president Fielding Wallace made an offer to Smith just three days before the scheduled start of the Southeastern Open. The Augusta tournament would be switched to a Saturday-Sunday affair, Smith would be given an early starting time on Sunday, and a plane would be provided at 2:00 p.m. for the four-hour flight to Washington, D.C., from where he could catch an overnight train to Boston. As an inducement, Smith would be guaranteed first-place prize money.

Smith accepted the offer, but undoubtedly wasn't at his best because of the harried travel schedule and the fact that he was playing on two courses that were totally unfamiliar to him (the first 36 holes were at Augusta Country Club and the final 36 at Forest Hills). He and Jones were paired in the first two rounds and a large gallery watched Jones take the lead with a 144 total while Smith was at 148. Smith teed off at 6:45 a.m. the second day, so early that he completed his third round before Jones even arrived at the course. Smith finished with a 297 total that earned him low-pro honors—but he was 13 strokes behind Jones's winning score.

Smith didn't even learn of the final result until the next morning in Boston. His flight to Washington was not uneventful. Those were still early days for air travel and the pilot of the single-engine plane, though he had been described by Wallace as "one of the best pilots in America," had never been north of Charlotte. He got lost when they got near Washington, and since the plane didn't have much fuel left he decided to land in a field on a farm to ask for directions. Fortunately, they were good directions, and Smith arrived safely in Washington, and Boston, on time.

More opportunities were ahead for Smith, as he toured Britain for a series of exhibitions with American pro Leo Diegel before playing in the 1930 British Open. Smith did better at the Open this time, finishing fourth, while Jones won the second leg of the Grand Slam, incidentally using a sand wedge that Smith had McCain make for him after Jones expressed his interest in the club in Savannah.

Then it was another boat trip across the ocean and a train ride to Minneapolis for the U.S. Open. Smith led through two rounds at Interlachen with a

142 total, but he couldn't keep pace on the 36-hole final day, shooting 76–74 to finish third while Jones took the trophy. Failure to win the U.S. or British Open or the PGA Championship was the only blemish on Smith's record— but he had plenty of company in not being able to beat Jones in an Open.

Smith finally had a chance to visit home after being on the road for twenty straight months, a period in which he had traveled an estimated 41,000 miles while playing in some 130 exhibitions and fifty tournaments. Horton insisted at the time that he felt fresh, but soon his body began to break down. It was physical woes more than anything that led to his decline over the next few years.

He began to experience back problems in the fall of 1930 and couldn't shake them for several years, and even then not completely. Smith had to cut down considerably on his practicing and also alter his swing because of his back. He stayed competitive thanks to his outstanding short game, but never again struck the ball as consistently as he did from 1928 to 1930.

CHAPTER 9

BEN HOGAN'S ULTIMATE TEST

JEFF MILLER

After Lloyd Mangrum christened the 1949 P.G.A. Tour season with a victory at the Los Angeles Open, Ben Hogan and Jimmy Demaret did their best to turn the rest of the month's schedule into a match race. Hogan won the Bing Crosby Pro-Am. Then they finished in a tie at Long Beach with Hogan taking the playoff 67 to 69. On to Phoenix and another playoff between them, won this time by Demaret, 67–70. There was no reason to believe things would be any different at the Tour's next stop, the Tucson Open, except that Hogan was headed back to Texas for a break before resuming play in San Antonio following a week's break.

If the Hogan-Demaret heroics weren't enough to gain the attention of golf fans across the country, Hogan was the cover story of the January 10, 1949, edition of *Time* magazine. The cover display offered the advice on which he based his career: "If you can't outplay them, outwork them." The extensive profile was written by Marshall Smith, who gave Hogan a taste of his own medicine while interviewing him. When Hogan was made aware of something that would be in the story that he wasn't enthusiastic about, he confronted Smith: "You're not going to say *that* in your story." To which the writer replied, "Look. Your game is golf. This story is my business. Let me handle it my way."

As January gave way to February, post-war tensions between the United States and the Soviet Union reached a new milepost. Soviet Premier Josef Stalin had offered President Harry S. Truman the opportunity to engage in disarmament talks—but only at a location behind the Iron Curtain because of his health. The administration recoiled; the new Secretary of State, Dean Acheson, replied in a news conference that the United States wasn't interested in such a summit. Stalin, Acheson said while referring to voluminous notes, had previously rejected invitations from the Americans to meet in Washington. Plus, Acheson added, such talks would involve many other countries and shouldn't be confined to simply the two well-armed superpowers.

Everything was going Hogan's way until the Greyhound bus coming at him in far west Texas knocked his Cadillac off the road, nearly killing him and his wife. Hogan skipped the Tucson tournament and left Phoenix on Tuesday, February 1, bound for Fort Worth, where that night "Jug" McSpaden was giving a golfing lecture at TCU's auditorium. The Hogans nearly covered half the distance in driving about seventy-five miles beyond El Paso. They reached the small town of Van Horn and called it a day, stopping at the El Capitan Motel. The following morning was frigidly cold across much of the Lone Star State, with snow covering parts of Waco and Austin. In Fort Worth, Oscar the Groundhog saw his shadow. Out in far west Texas, there was early morning fog and at least a slight glaze of ice on U.S. Highway 80, the main route between El Paso and Dallas-Fort Worth. The Hogans were back on the road at eight looking at almost another full day's drive before arriving home. They had not gone far when Hogan told his wife, "I think we've got a flat tire." He pulled off the two-lane road, determined there was nothing wrong with the tires, and continued driving. Having noticed ice on the road for the first time that morning, he told Valerie that he'd drive slightly slower.

Only a few minutes after the Hogans were rolling again, the glow of headlights—right in front of their Cadillac—came seeping through the fog. It was a bus in their lane, the driver in the midst of passing a truck. The driver, Alvin Logan, had spent about six miles behind the truck and decided this stretch of winding, dipping road was suitable for trying to make the pass. As the Cadillac and Greyhound bore down on each other, the Hogans were crossing over a culvert with a concrete barrier that prevented Hogan from swerving to the right. Valerie screamed, "Honey, he's going to hit us!" Hogan instinctively threw himself over his wife's lap to shield her from the impending collision. Had he remained in the driver's seat, the impact of the steering column being thrust back into him surely would have killed him. The car was knocked well off the road and into a ditch. Hogan was concerned the Cadillac would catch fire and yelled for Valerie to get out of the car. As they both managed to escape the vehicle, passersby began to come to their aid. With people frantically concerned for the Hogans' welfare, it somehow took about an hour for someone to summon an ambulance. Hogan tried to assure people that he was fine, though it was already obvious that he'd suffered at the very least a broken ankle and an injured left leg. While they were waiting to make the trip to the Hotel Dieu Hospital back in El Paso, Hogan kept asking about his golf clubs, which were in the trunk of the Cadillac. Valerie asked police on the scene to please get the clubs and send them along with them. It turned out Hogan had sustained a double fracture of the pelvis, a fractured collar bone and a chipped rib in addition to the leg and foot issues. As for Valerie, her injuries were limited to some bruises and a black eye thanks to her husband's quick thinking.

Hogan initially recovered at an encouraging pace in El Paso. Royal Hogan, who rushed there upon hearing the news, indicated to hometown reporters that his brother would be transferred home within a matter of days. But the timetable soon changed when Hogan suffered a significant setback; blood clots worked their way from his injured left leg into his lungs. For the first time since the initial aftermath of the crash, there was legitimate concern for Hogan's life. A specialist in vascular surgery was contacted in New Orleans, but he couldn't immediately get a seat on a commercial plane bound for El Paso because of the ongoing Mardi Gras celebration. Valerie then recalled one of the visitors in Hogan's first days in the hospital was a brigadier general stationed nearby. She contacted him at midnight and, with his help, a plane was sent to bring Dr. Alton Ochsner to Hotel Dieu. The operation was a success, but Hogan remained hospitalized in El Paso for two months and never fully recovered from the leg injuries. They would require daily attention—massages, baths and extensive leg wrappings—for years to come. The Hogans were overwhelmed with well-wishers and expressions of people's concern for Ben while in El Paso. Valerie told the *Fort Worth Star-Telegram* the episode had made her husband realize how much people cared for him.

By the time the Hogans rode a train to Fort Worth in early April, no one was possibly considering Hogan would play P.G.A. Tour golf again—except for Hogan himself. Maybe he doubted he could do it or maybe he was building his own target for motivation when he told reporters, "Don't waste your time writing about me. People are tired of hearing about Ben Hogan. They're interested in the guys who are playing now. It won't be long until they forget all about me." His return to golf came as captain of the United States' 1949 Ryder Cup team, which retained the trophy with a 7-to-5 victory at the Ganton Golf Club in Scarborough, England. By that autumn, he was prepared to take steps to return to the game. In early November, he was on the practice range at Colonial. About a month later, Hogan played his first round of golf, with the aid of a cart, since the playoff in Phoenix about eleven months earlier. News of the Saturday afternoon jaunt around Colonial on a chilly, cloudy day appeared in the next day's *Star-Telegram* without a writer's byline and beneath a headline that began with the word FLASH! "I didn't hit them very well," Hogan allowed. His playing partner, Ridglea pro Raymond Gafford, offered that Hogan hit them "well enough." That following day's *Press* noted Hogan played another eighteen holes at Colonial that Sunday, shot 71 and 72 for the weekend and complained of being "a little tired."

His next step—literally—was to complete a round while walking, which he did a week later. His goal was to enter the first event of the 1950 season, the $15,000 Los Angeles Open scheduled for Friday through Monday, January 6–9. About the same time that Hogan was first playing eighteen holes without a cart, representatives of the L.A. event asked him if he could come out to the tournament and serve as the honorary starter. A few days later, the Hogans were on a train headed to California. He piqued the interest of reporters at the station in Fort Worth by indicating he was interested in actually playing at Riviera Country Club, where he won the 1948 National Open. At least one Hogan fan was certain he would return to tournament play—Alton

Ochsner, the surgeon who saved his life. "Ben has the kind of determination that leaves no doubt as to the ultimate outcome," Ochsner was quoted in the *Star-Telegram* during the Los Angeles tournament. "Doctors not infrequently recognize this will in patients, but in few people has it ever been more evident than in Hogan."

Oh, Hogan indeed played; his performance at the 1950 Los Angeles Open would have been the story of the year on the Tour were it not for his later heroics on a grander stage. The four practice rounds that he played totaled three shots less than Mangrum's winning score a year earlier, though he brought along a chair for resting between holes. "It's all a question of my legs," he said after a practice round. "They've been tiring in the latter parts of rounds." Among those who played practice rounds with Hogan was Cary Middlecoff, the defending U.S. Open champion. "He pinned our ears back," reported Middlecoff, the former dentist who gave up his practice to play professional golf. At one point, Hogan told his playing partners that his legs hurt like hell and then deposited his next shot twenty feet from the pin.

Hogan opened with a 2-over-par 73 that left him five shots behind leader Ed Furgol. As per his fears, his play withered along with his legs on the back nine. Hogan also appeared unusually distracted by things that previously didn't affect him, like noises from a construction crew working on a home site above the seventh green. But he then incredibly fired off three consecutive rounds of 69 on Saturday, Monday, and Tuesday (with Sunday's play rained out) and no longer seemed impacted by potential agitations such as an amateur photographer facing down his putting line. Hogan tied for first place at 4-under 280 with Sam Snead, who required a 15-foot birdie putt on his seventy-second hole to force the playoff. An exhausted Hogan obviously didn't welcome the prospect of another grueling eighteen holes. "I'm awfully tired," he told reporters. "I wish I didn't have to play tomorrow."

Hogan didn't have to play tomorrow. More rain washed out the Wednesday playoff and, with the popular Bing Crosby Pro-Am scheduled to start up the coast on Friday, the decision was made to reschedule the L.A. playoff until *after* the Crosby event. Hogan played at the three-round Pebble Beach tournament, where he was the defending champion. He didn't experience the same success that he enjoyed at Riviera. His best round there was "only" a par-72—still remarkable given what had happened to him in the previous year—and finished in a tie for nineteenth place. Byron Nelson, playing in a Tour event for the first time since the previous May, shot 4-over 148 for two rounds and withdrew.

Snead was among four players who tied for first at the Crosby—missing an eight-foot putt that would have claimed the championship—and tournament officials didn't bother with a playoff; all four were declared winners. Hogan was glad to be leaving chilly northern California, but the forecast on Monday called for showers in Los Angeles on Wednesday. The rain held off, but the combatants were greeted at Riviera by low fog. The proceedings began with a dismal omen for Hogan when his initial tee shot went hooking out of bounds. Snead led by two shots after two holes and maintained that edge through the front nine. He did the same coming home, holding even par while Hogan shot 2-over to win 72 to 76. "I was lousy," Hogan growled afterward. Snead countered: "He was terrific. He's the same old Hogan. He scares you to death." There was an awkward episode on no. 13 when Snead became impatient with the amount of time that Hogan was taking on putts and walked off the green while Hogan was putting. Years later, Snead told the *Los Angeles Times* that he thought Hogan purposely took that much time, trying to drain his opponent's momentum. For those in Dallas–Fort Worth who wished to watch a delayed telecast of the playoff, WBAP-TV provided that opportunity the following Sunday night—sponsored by Royal Hogan's office supply store.

Hogan skipped the Long Beach tournament but played in Phoenix, where organizers renamed the 1950 event the Ben Hogan Open; following a first-round 65, he faded and finished in a tie for twentieth place. Hogan didn't make another start for almost two months, appearing in the non-Tour Seminole Pro-Am in Palm Beach, Florida, in mid-March. He was working out of a hole, opening with a 79, and could manage only a tie for twenty-fourth place. Then it was on to a triumphant return to Augusta. Incredibly, Hogan stood only two shots out of the lead heading to the final round. But he closed with a 4-over 76 leaving him in fourth place, five shots behind three-time Masters winner Demaret.

If there was any animosity between Hogan and Snead given the events of the Los Angeles Open, it didn't prevent Hogan from showing up for Snead's Greenbriar Open a few weeks later. The event featured only twenty-five players, and Hogan shot a 21-under 259 to beat the host pro by ten shots. Hogan's plan had been to follow the West Virginia stop with a trip to the Western Open, but he decided against that. Next up would be another emotional experience—as if any appearance at this stage wouldn't be—returning to Marvin Leonard's course. It appeared the Colonial National Invitational Tournament couldn't be played without Bantam Ben; the 1949 event that was scheduled while Hogan was convalescing was cancelled because of flooding. At Hogan's homecoming in May 1950, Snead gained a measure of revenge by winning on Hogan's home layout. Hogan was hardly a disappointment, though, placing third. The following day, he caught a train for Philadelphia to play in two weeks in the U.S. Open at Merion Golf Club, where he would be required to play thirty-six holes in a single day for the first time in his return.

In the days leading up to the National Open, Snead acknowledged to the *Richmond News Leader* that Hogan was on his mind—either that or he was writing another chapter of gamesmanship. "The man who wins it will have to beat me," Snead said. "I'm not playing sensationally, but I'm playing well. I actually think Hogan is the man who might make some trouble. He's the man I've got to beat." During Hogan's practice rounds at Merion, he made the decision to replace his usual 7-iron with a 1-iron after determining there were no 7-iron shots on the historic East Course. Like it was at Riviera, the issue of Hogan's durability seemed to be the most popular topic of pretournament repartee. Gene Sarazen, the 1934 Open winner, was forthright if not polite in his assessment: "If they were going to play it without walking—just hitting the shots—I would pick Ben without hesitation. But, unfortunately, he will have to walk."

For at least a day, events pushed the story of the historic Hogan come-back to the back pages. Lee Mackey, Jr., a 26-year-old from Birmingham, Alabama, with no professional wins, broke both the course record and the National Open one-round mark in Thursday's first round by one-putting ten holes and firing a 6-under-par 64. Hogan opened with a 2-over-par 72, recovering from a rickety start shooting 39 on the front nine. When reporters sought an explanation from Mackey for his implausible taming of Merion, he replied, "I guess I just got lucky." Alas, he failed to pack luck into his bag the next day; he stumbled through an 11-over 81 that took him out of conten-tion. Hogan's second-day score of 1-under 69 was shot with a midmorning tee time that enabled him to miss the most scorching portion of a Philadel-phia day that reached a humid 95 degrees, though he did experience some cramping at the no. 12 hole. His overall 1-over 141 placed him only two shots behind leader "Dutch" Harrison in fifth place.

For Saturday's 36-hole finale viewed by a National Open record 12,500 spectators, Hogan was paired with Middlecoff going off at 9:30 a.m. and 2 p.m. As would be the case for the rest of Hogan's career, early starting times were problematic because of the hours of preparation required for getting his legs ready for competition. He completed the morning round in 2-over 72, putting him two behind Mangrum and one behind Harrison. On the twelfth hole of the afternoon round, owning a three-stroke advantage, Hogan suffered through more than cramping this time around; he grimaced after striking his tee shot and began to stagger, grabbing onto a friend to prevent himself from falling, and went on to bogey the hole. Years later, Hogan told the *Star-Telegram* that his legs had turned to stone and he wasn't certain he could finish. For the balance of the round, Hogan's putts were extracted from the cups by either his caddie or Middlecoff's. And then after playing the thir-teenth, according to separate interviews that Hogan gave years later, the pain was so great he was resigned to the fact that he couldn't finish—only to have his caddie insist on meeting him at the no. 14 tee box.

Suffering bogeys on nos. 15 and 17 because of putting issues, Hogan trudged to the par-4, 458-yard eighteenth having lost a three-shot lead over six holes. He needed a par to force a three-way playoff with Mangrum and George Fazio, the latter a hometown boy whose two Tour triumphs consisted of the 1946 Canadian Open and the '47 Crosby. After a tee shot that nestled in the middle of the fairway more than 200 yards from the pin, he called upon the 1-iron that he'd subbed into his bag just before play began. His approach, captured in the renowned photograph shot by Hy Peskin for *Life,* carried the treacherous rough lurking right of the fairway and in front of the green and landed just short of the green but carried up onto the putting surface about forty feet from the flag stick. His first putt rolled four feet past the hole; he quickly struck the return putt to earn his par for the hole—a 4-over 74 for the round—and another day's play. (Hogan told long-time golf writer Charles Price that he struck the putt hastily because his legs hurt so much he was eager to end the round and get off his feet. On the way back to his hotel afterward, Hogan became sick to his stomach.) In the chaos of excitement in the aftermath of the drama, the club that Hogan used to reach the eighteenth green—years later, debate raged over whether it was his 1-iron or 2-iron—was pilfered from his golf bag. If it *wasn't* the 1-iron, the granite marker placed in the fairway to honor the achievement is in error.

Valerie Hogan feared her husband couldn't endure another eighteen holes that Sunday. Wasn't she pleasantly surprised, as she recalled for Dave Anderson, when Ben awoke that morning and exclaimed, "Isn't it a nice day?" In the lobby of the Barclay Hotel, reporters diligently checked on Hogan's condition—and some all but rooted him on as he and Valerie left for the 30-minute drive to Merion. Hogan's day would ordinarily have started much earlier with a morning tee time for the playoff, but state blue laws prohibited starting before 1 p.m. In the three-way battle, Hogan took his first lead on the par-4 seventh when his approach landed only four feet from the pin and he converted the birdie putt. He gave back the stroke with a bogey on the eighth hole, and Hogan and Mangrum stood even following nine holes. Hogan was back on top through twelve holes, his even-par round providing him a one-shot lead over both of his competitors. When Fazio and Mangrum each bogeyed the par-4 fourteenth, Hogan enjoyed a two-stroke cushion with four holes to play. Mangrum managed to birdie no. 15 to get back within one.

Then came the infamous turn of events at no. 16. With Mangrum preparing to putt, he unwittingly committed a rules violation when he addressed his ball, then picked it up to blow a bug off it. He was assessed a two-stroke penalty; prior to 1960, U.S.G.A. rules allowed players to mark and pick up their ball on the green only when the ball interfered with another player. Mangrum later stated he was initially unaware of the ruling, thinking he'd putted for a par. It was only in the tee area on no. 17 that U.S.G.A. official

This plaque sits on the 18th fairway at Merion East Golf Course in commemoration of Hogan's 1950 feat. *(Bert Stewart, via Wikimedia Commons)*

Ike Grainger explained to him what happened. Hogan was ahead by three shots with two holes to play but played like a man needing to shoot a birdie. Which he did on no. 17, thanks to a 50-foot uphill putt. On no. 18, missing the club that he used for his second shot on Saturday afternoon, Hogan played a 5-iron—and sent the ball over the green. His chip back came to rest seven feet from the cup, and a one-putt gave him a 1-under 69 to Mangrum's 73 and Fazio's 75. The crowd around the green was prepared to hoist the victorious Hogan on their shoulders but was halted by the local constabulary. Hogan admitted to reporters that winning the 1950 Open topped even his first Open victory in Los Angeles two years earlier: "This was my biggest thrill. And I'm awfully glad that those two strokes Lloyd lost on the sixteenth green penalty didn't make the difference." One of the wags later mentioned something about retirement. "Retire?" Hogan replied with a laugh. "I love golf, and I'll never quit it competitively."

Hogan poses with his 1950 US Open trophy *(AP Photo)*

PART TWO

LESSONS FOR LIFE

CHAPTER 10

GOLF AS A YOUTH

FRANCIS OUIMET

It was as a school-boy golfer that I first had that feeling of satisfaction which comes in winning a tournament, and it was as a school-boy golfer that I learned a few things which perhaps may be useful to some boys who are pupils in school now and who are interested in golf. It was in 1908 that I took part for the first time in an interscholastic tournament, at the Wollaston Golf Club, and I may as well say, right here, that I did not win the title; the fact is that I barely qualified, my 85 being only one stroke better than the worst score in the championship qualifying division. The best score was 74, which I must say was extraordinarily good for such a course as that on which the event was played. It is a fine score there today for any golfer, even in the ranks of the men. In my first round of match play, fortune favored me, only to make me the victim of its caprices in the second round, when I was defeated two up and one to play by the eventual winner of the championship title, Carl Anderson. It was inability to run down putts of about three feet in length which cost me that match, and, to my sorrow, I have passed through that same experience more than once since leaving school. But what I recollect distinctly about that match, aside from my troubles on the putting-greens, was that I felt nervous from the start, for it was my first "big" match. I mention this because it has its own little lesson, which is that the chances of winning are less when the thought of winning is so much on the mind as to affect the nerves.

It was as a school-boy that Ouimet first felt the satisfaction of winning a tournament. *(Andrew Penner, via iStock)*

In 1909 I won the championship of the Greater Boston Interscholastic Golf Association, the tournament being played at the Commonwealth Country Club, Newton, Massachusetts. Only one match was at all close, that one going to the sixteenth green. The final, at thirty-six holes, I won by ten up and nine to play. In that tournament I learned a lesson invaluable, which was to avoid trying to play every shot equally well with my opponent. In other words, there were boys in that tournament who were vastly my superiors in long hitting. Frequently they were reaching the green in two shots where I required three, or else they were getting there with a drive and a mashie shot where I required two long shots. But, fortunately, I was of a temperament at that time which enabled me to go along my own way, never trying to hit the ball beyond my natural strength in order to go as far as my opponent, and making up for lack of distance by accuracy of direction and better putting. My advice to any boy is to play his own game, irrespective of what his opponent does. This does not mean, of course, that a boy should lose his ambition to improve his game, or that he should be content with moderate distance when he might be able to do better. But the time for striving to do better is not when ambition is aroused merely through the desire to win some one match or to outhit some opponent. The average boy or man who strives in some one match to hit the ball harder than he does normally generally finds that, instead of getting greater distance, he is only spoiling his natural game. Then, the harder he tries, the worse he gets. Greater distance on the drive, as well as accuracy in all departments of the game, comes through practice and natural development, rather than through the extra efforts of some one round.

In that tournament at the Commonwealth Country Club, which gave me the first championship title which I ever held in golf, there were a number of players who subsequently have achieved successes in athletic lines, several of them having become prominent for their skill in golf. Among these was Heinrich Schmidt, of Worcester, Massachusetts, who in the spring of 1913, made such a great showing in the British amateur championship. Even at that time, "Heinie," as we called him, was a more than ordinarily good golfer, and he was looked upon as one of the possible winners of the championship. It was one of his Worcester team-mates, Arthur Knight, who put him out of the running, in a match that went two extra holes. "Heinie's" twin brother, Karl, who looked so much like him that it was difficult to tell the two apart, also was in the tournament, and among others were the late Dana Wingate, afterwards captain of the Harvard varsity baseball nine; Forrester Ainsworth, half-back on the Yale football eleven in 1913; and Fletcher Gill, who later played on the Williams College golf team.

The following year, 1910, I was honored with election to the presidency of the Greater Boston Interscholastic Golf Association, which did not, however, help me to retain the championship title, for that year the winner was Arthur Knight, of Worcester.

This interesting tournament was played on the links of the Woodland Golf Club at Auburndale, Massachusetts, and in the qualifying round I was medalist, with a score of 77. Singularly enough, I had that same score in winning my match of the first round, and also had a 77 in the second round; but on that occasion it was not good enough to win; for Francis Mahan, one of

Ouimet, pictured here in 1932, well after his school-boy days, reflected on lessons that he believed youth golfers should be learning. *(Courtesy of the Boston Public Library, Leslie Jones Collection)*

my team-mates from Brookline High School, was around with a brilliant 73, whereby he won by three up and two to play. It was beautiful golf for a boy (for a man, either, as far as that goes), and the loss of the title, under such circumstances, left nothing for me to regret. It always has struck me that for any one who truly loves the game of golf, there is even a pleasure in being defeated when you have played first-class golf yourself, and have been beaten only because your opponent has played even better. It certainly was so in that case, and I was sorry that Mahan could not keep up the gait in his other matches. He was beaten by the eventual winner of the tournament, Arthur Knight, in the semi-final round, Knight winning the thirty-six-hole final by two up and one to play from R. W. Gleason, later a member of the Williams College team.

From my own experiences in school-boy golf, I should be an enthusiastic supporter of any movement tending to make the game a greater factor in the athletic life of school-boys or, for that matter, in the colleges. I do think, however, that it should come under more direct supervision of older heads, and that boys should be taught not only how to play the game, but that they should have impressed upon them the fact that it is a game that demands absolute honesty.

I have known instances where, in school-boy tournaments, scores have been returned which were surprisingly low, and there have been occasions when such scores, appearing in print, have brought a tinge of suspicion upon the boys returning them. Such instances would be rare if proper methods were taken to explain to the boys that golf is a game which puts them strictly on their honor. They should be taught to realize that winning is not everything in the game; that a prize won through trickery, either in turning in a wrong score or moving the ball to give it a more desirable position, gives no lasting pleasure. Any boy winning a prize by such methods would in later life want to have it out of sight. Every time he looked at it, he would have a feeling of contempt for himself for having adopted dishonest methods. Under proper supervision, golf can be made a great agency in the schools for the development of character; a game which will teach the boy to be honest with himself and with others.

CHAPTER 11

THE STORY OF THE LONG HOLE

P. G. WODEHOUSE

The young man, as he sat filling his pipe in the clubhouse smoking room, was inclined to be bitter.

"If there's one thing that gives me a pain squarely in the centre of the gizzard," he burst out, breaking a silence that had lasted for some minutes, "it's a golf-lawyer. They oughtn't to be allowed on the links."

The Oldest Member, who had been meditatively putting himself outside a cup of tea and a slice of seed-cake, raised his white eyebrows.

"The Law," he said, "is an honourable profession. Why should its practitioners be restrained from indulgence in the game of games?"

"I don't mean actual lawyers," said the young man, his acerbity mellowing a trifle under the influence of tobacco. "I mean the blighters whose best club is the book of rules. You know the sort of excrescences. Every time you think you've won a hole, they dig out Rule 853, section two, sub-section four, to prove that you've disqualified yourself by having an ingrowing toe nail. Well, take my case." The young man's voice was high and plaintive. "I go out with that man Hemmingway to play an ordinary friendly round—nothing depending on it except a measly ball—and on the seventh he pulls me up and claims the hole simply because I happened to drop my niblick in the bunker. Oh, well, a tick's a tick, and there's nothing more to say, I suppose."

The Sage shook his head.

"Rules are rules, my boy, and must be kept. It is odd that you should have brought up this subject, for only a moment before you came in I was thinking of a somewhat curious match which ultimately turned upon a question of the rule-book. It is true that, as far as the actual prize was concerned, it made little difference. But perhaps I had better tell you the whole story from the beginning."

The young man shifted uneasily in his chair.

"Well, you know, I've had a pretty rotten time this afternoon already—"

"I will call my story," said the Sage, tranquilly, " 'The Long Hole', for it involved the playing of what I am inclined to think must be the longest hole in the history of golf. In its beginnings the story may remind you of one I once told you about Peter Willard and James Todd, but you will find that it develops in quite a different manner. Ralph Bingham. . . ."

"I half promised to go and see a man—"

"But I will begin at the beginning," said the Sage. "I see that you are all impatience to hear the full details."

* * * * *

Ralph Bingham and Arthur Jukes (said the Oldest Member) had never been friends—their rivalry was too keen to admit of that—but it was not till Amanda Trivett came to stay here that a smouldering distaste for each other burst out into the flames of actual enmity. It is ever so. One of the poets, whose name I cannot recall, has a passage, which I am unable at the moment to remember, in one of his works, which for the time being has slipped my mind, which hits off admirably this age-old situation. The gist of his remarks is that lovely woman rarely fails to start something. In the weeks that followed her arrival, being in the same room with the two men was like dropping in on a reunion of Capulets and Montagues.

You see, Ralph and Arthur were so exactly equal in their skill on the links that life for them had for some time past resolved itself into a silent, bitter struggle in which first one, then the other, gained some slight advantage. If Ralph won the May medal by a stroke, Arthur would be one ahead in the June competition, only to be nosed out again in July. It was a state of affairs which, had they been men of a more generous stamp, would have bred a mutual respect, esteem, and even love. But I am sorry to say that, apart from their golf, which was in a class of its own as far as this neighbourhood was concerned, Ralph Bingham and Arthur Jukes were a sorry pair—and yet, mark you, far from lacking in mere superficial good looks. They were handsome fellows, both of them, and well aware of the fact; and when Amanda Trivett came to stay they simply straightened their ties, twirled their moustaches, and expected her to do the rest.

But there they were disappointed. Perfectly friendly though she was to both of them, the lovelight was conspicuously absent from her beautiful eyes. And it was not long before each had come independently to a solution of this mystery. It was plain to them that the whole trouble lay in the fact that each neutralized the other's attractions. Arthur felt that, if he could only have a clear field, all would be over except the sending out of the wedding invitations; and Ralph was of the opinion that, if he could just call on the girl one evening without finding the place all littered up with Arthur, his natural charms would swiftly bring home the bacon. And, indeed, it was true that they had no rivals except themselves. It happened at the moment that Woodhaven was very short of eligible bachelors. We marry young in this delightful spot, and all the likely men were already paired off. It seemed that, if Amanda Trivett intended to get married, she would have to select either Ralph Bingham or Arthur Jukes. A dreadful choice.

* * * * *

It had not occurred to me at the outset that my position in the affair would be anything closer than that of a detached and mildly interested spectator. Yet it was to me that Ralph came in his hour of need. When I returned home one evening, I found that my man had brought him in and laid him on the mat in my sitting-room.

I offered him a chair and a cigar, and he came to the point with commendable rapidity.

"Leigh," he said, directly he had lighted his cigar, "is too small for Arthur Jukes and myself."

"Ah, you have been talking it over and decided to move?" I said, delighted. "I think you are perfectly right. Leigh is over-built. Men like you and Jukes need a lot of space. Where do you think of going?"

"I'm not going."

"But I thought you said—"

"What I meant was that the time has come when one of us must leave."

"Oh, only one of you?" It was something, of course, but I confess I was disappointed, and I think my disappointment must have shown in my voice; for he looked at me, surprised.

"Surely you wouldn't mind Jukes going?" he said.

"Why, certainly not. He really is going, is he?"

A look of saturnine determination came into Ralph's face.

"He is. He thinks he isn't, but he is."

I failed to understand him, and said so. He looked cautiously about the room, as if to reassure himself that he could not be overheard.

"I suppose you've noticed," he said, "the disgusting way that man Jukes has been hanging round Miss Trivett, boring her to death?"

"I have seen them together sometimes."

"I love Amanda Trivett!" said Ralph.

"Poor girl!" I sighed.

"I beg your pardon?"

"Poor girl!" I said. "I mean, to have Arthur Jukes hanging round her."

"That's just what I think," said Ralph Bingham. "And that's why we're going to play this match."

"What match?"

"This match we've decided to play. I want you to act as one of the judges, to go along with Jukes and see that he doesn't play any of his tricks. You know what he is! And in a vital match like this—"

"How much are you playing for?"

"The whole world!"

"I beg your pardon?"

"The whole world. It amounts to that. The loser is to leave Leigh for good, and the winner stays on and marries Amanda Trivett. We have arranged all the details. Rupert Bailey will accompany me, acting as the other judge."

"And you want me to go round with Jukes?"

"Not round," said Ralph Bingham. "Along."

"What is the distinction?"

"We are not going to play a round. Only one hole."

"Sudden death, eh?"

"Not so very sudden. It's a longish hole. We start on the first tee here and hole out in the town in the doorway of the Majestic Hotel in Royal Square. A distance, I imagine, of about sixteen miles."

I was revolted. About that time a perfect epidemic of freak matches had broken out in the club, and I had strongly opposed them from the start. George Willis had begun it by playing a medal round with the pro, George's first nine against the pro's complete eighteen. After that came the contest between Herbert Widgeon and Montague Brown, the latter, a twenty-four handicap man, being entitled to shout "Boo!" three times during the round at moments selected by himself. There had been many more of these degrading travesties on the sacred game, and I had writhed to see them. Playing freak golf-matches is to my mind like ragging a great classical melody. But of the whole collection this one, considering the sentimental interest and the magnitude of the stakes, seemed to me the most terrible. My face, I imagine, betrayed my disgust, for Bingham attempted extenuation.

"It's the only way," he said. "You know how Jukes and I are on the links. We are as level as two men can be. This, of course is due to his extraordinary luck. Everybody knows that he is the world's champion fluker. I, on the other hand, invariably have the worst luck. The consequence is that in an ordinary round it is always a toss-up which of us wins. The test we propose will eliminate luck. After sixteen miles of give-and-take play, I am certain—that is to say, the better man is certain to be ahead. That is what I meant when I said

Arthur Jukes and Ralph Bingham had arranged the details. They'd play a long hole, of about sixteen miles, to determine who would win and marry Amanda Trivett. *(StAgur Karlsson, courtesy of iStock)*

that Arthur Jukes would shortly be leaving Leigh. Well, may I take it that you will consent to act as one of the judges?"

I considered. After all, the match was likely to be historic, and one always feels tempted to hand one's name down to posterity.

"Very well," I said.

"Excellent. You will have to keep a sharp eye on Jukes, I need scarcely remind you. You will, of course, carry a book of the rules in your pocket and refer to them when you wish to refresh your memory. We start at daybreak, for, if we put it off till later, the course at the other end might be somewhat congested when we reached it. We want to avoid publicity as far as possible. If I took a full iron and hit a policeman, it would excite a remark."

"It would. I can tell you the exact remark which it would excite."

"We will take bicycles with us, to minimize the fatigue of covering the distance. Well, I am glad that we have your co-operation. At daybreak tomorrow on the first tee, and don't forget to bring your rule-book."

* * * * *

The atmosphere brooding over the first tee when I reached it on the following morning, somewhat resembled that of a duelling-ground in the days when these affairs were sealed with rapiers or pistols. Rupert Bailey, an old friend of mine, was the only cheerful member of the party. I am never at my best in the early morning, and the two rivals glared at each other with silent sneers. I had never supposed till that moment that men ever really sneered at one another outside the movies, but these two were indisputably doing so. They were in the mood when men say "Pshaw!"

They tossed for the honour, and Arthur Jukes, having won, drove off with a fine ball that landed well down the course. Ralph Bingham, having teed up, turned to Rupert Bailey.

"Go down on to the fairway of the seventeenth," he said. "I want you to mark my ball."

Rupert stared.

Ralph was not concerned about his shot landing in the lake. He had a boat ready for that. *(Otmar Winterleitner, via iStock)*

"The seventeenth!"

"I am going to take that direction," said Ralph, pointing over the trees.

"But that will land your second or third shot in the lake."

"I have provided for that. I have a fiat-bottomed boat moored close by the sixteenth green. I shall use a mashie-niblick and chip my ball aboard, row across to the other side, chip it ashore, and carry on. I propose to go across country as far as Woodfield. I think it will save me a stroke or two."

I gasped. I had never before realized the man's devilish cunning. His tactics gave him a flying start. Arthur, who had driven straight down the course, had as his objective the high road, which adjoins the waste ground beyond the first green. Once there, he would play the orthodox game by driving his ball along till he reached the bridge. While Arthur was winding along the high road, Ralph would have cut off practically two sides of a triangle. And it was hopeless for Arthur to imitate his enemy's tactics now. From where his ball lay he would have to cross a wide tract of marsh in order to reach the seventeenth fairway—an impossible feat. And, even if it had been feasible, he had no boat to take him across the water.

He uttered a violent protest. He was an unpleasant young man, almost—it seems absurd to say so, but almost as unpleasant as Ralph Bingham; yet at the moment I am bound to say I sympathized with him.

"What are you doing?" he demanded. "You can't play fast and loose with the rules like that."

"To what rule do you refer?" said Ralph, coldly.

"Well, that bally boat of yours is a hazard, isn't it? And you can't row a hazard about all over the place."

"Why not?"

The simple question seemed to take Arthur Jukes aback.

"Why not?" he repeated. "Why not? Well, you can't. That's why."

"There is nothing in the rules," said Ralph Bingham, "against moving a hazard. If a hazard can be moved without disturbing the ball, you are at liberty, I gather, to move it wherever you please. Besides, what is all this about moving hazards? I have a perfect right to go for a morning row, haven't I? If I were to ask my doctor, he would probably actually recommend it. I am going to row my boat across the sound. If it happens to have my ball on board, that is not my affair. I shall not disturb my ball, and I shall play it from where it lies. Am I right in saying that the rules enact that the ball shall be played from where it lies?"

We admitted that it was.

"Very well, then," said Ralph Bingham. "Don't let us waste any more time. We will wait for you at Woodfield."

He addressed his ball, and drove a beauty over the trees. It flashed out of sight in the direction of the seventeenth tee. Arthur and I made our way down the hill to play our second.

* * * * *

It is a curious trait of the human mind that, however little personal interest one may have in the result, it is impossible to prevent oneself taking sides in any event of a competitive nature. I had embarked on this affair in a purely neutral spirit, not caring which of the two won and only sorry that both could not lose. Yet, as the morning wore on, I found myself almost unconsciously becoming distinctly pro-Jukes. I did not like the man. I objected to his face, his manners, and the colour of his tie. Yet there was something in the dogged way in which he struggled against adversity which touched me and won my grudging support. Many men, I felt, having been so outmanoeuvred at the start, would have given up the contest in despair; but Arthur Jukes, for all his defects, had the soul of a true golfer. He declined to give up. In grim silence he hacked his ball through the rough till he reached the high road; and then, having played twenty-seven, set himself resolutely to propel it on its long journey.

It was a lovely morning, and, as I bicycled along, keeping a fatherly eye on Arthur's activities, I realized for the first time in my life the full meaning of that exquisite phrase of Coleridge: "Clothing the palpable and familiar/ With golden exhalations of the dawn." For in the pellucid air everything seemed weirdly beautiful, even Arthur Jukes's heather-mixture knickerbockers, of which hitherto I had never approved. The sun gleamed on their seat, as he bent to make his shots, in a cheerful and almost a poetic way. The birds were singing gaily in the hedgerows, and such was my uplifted state that I, too, burst into song, until Arthur petulantly desired me to refrain, on the plea that, though he yielded to no man in his enjoyment of farmyard imitations in their proper place, I put him off his stroke. And so we passed through Bayside in silence and started to cover that long stretch of road which ends in the railway bridge and the gentle descent into Woodfield.

Arthur was not doing badly. He was at least keeping them straight. And in the circumstances straightness was to be preferred to distance. Soon after leaving Little Hadley he had become ambitious and had used his brassey with disastrous results, slicing his fifty-third into the rough on the right of the road. It had taken him ten with the niblick to get back on to the car tracks, and this had taught him prudence.

He was now using his putter for every shot, and, except when he got trapped in the cross-lines at the top of the hill just before reaching Bayside, he had been in no serious difficulties. He was playing a nice easy game, getting the full face of the putter on to each shot.

At the top of the slope that drops down into Woodfield High Street he paused.

"I think I might try my brassey again here," he said. "I have a nice lie."

"Is it wise?" I said.

He looked down the hill.

"What I was thinking," he said, "was that with it I might wing that man Bingham. I see he is standing right out in the middle of the fairway."

I followed his gaze. It was perfectly true. Ralph Bingham was leaning on his bicycle in the roadway, smoking a cigarette. Even at this distance one could detect the man's disgustingly complacent expression. Rupert Bailey was sitting with his back against the door of the Woodfield Garage, looking rather used up. He was a man who liked to keep himself clean and tidy, and it was plain that the cross-country trip had done him no good. He seemed to be scraping mud off his face. I learned later that he had had the misfortune to fall into a ditch just beyond Bayside.

"No," said Arthur. "On second thoughts, the safe game is the one to play. I'll stick to the putter."

We dropped down the hill, and presently came up with the opposition. I had not been mistaken in thinking that Ralph Bingham looked complacent. The man was smirking.

"Playing three hundred and ninety-six," he said, as we drew near. "How are you?"

I consulted my score-card.

"We have played a snappy seven hundred and eleven," I said.

Ralph exulted openly. Rupert Bailey made no comment. He was too busy with the alluvial deposits on his person.

"Perhaps you would like to give up the match?" said Ralph to Arthur.

"Tchah!" said Arthur.

"Might just as well."

"Pah!" said Arthur.

"You can't win now."

"Pshaw!" said Arthur.

I am aware that Arthur's dialogue might have been brighter, but he had been through a trying time.

Rupert Bailey sidled up to me.

"I'm going home," he said.

"Nonsense!" I replied. "You are in an official capacity. You must stick to your post. Besides, what could be nicer than a pleasant morning ramble?"

"Pleasant morning ramble my number nine foot!" he replied, peevishly. "I want to get back to civilization and set an excavating party with pickaxes to work on me."

"You take too gloomy a view of the matter. You are a little dusty. Nothing more."

"And it's not only the being buried alive that I mind. I cannot stick Ralph Bingham much longer."

"You have found him trying?"

"Trying! Why, after I had fallen into that ditch and was coming up for the third time, all the man did was simply to call to me to admire an infernal iron shot he had just made. No sympathy, mind you! Wrapped up in himself. Why don't you make your man give up the match? He can't win."

"I refuse to admit it. Much may happen between here and Royal Square."

I have seldom known a prophecy more swiftly fulfilled. At this moment the doors of the Woodfield Garage opened and a small car rolled out with a grimy young man in a sweater at the wheel. He brought the machine out into the road, and alighted and went back into the garage, where we heard him shouting unintelligibly to someone in the rear premises. The car remained puffing and panting against the kerb.

Engaged in conversation with Rupert Bailey, I was paying little attention to this evidence of an awakening world, when suddenly I heard a hoarse, triumphant cry from Arthur Jukes, and, turned, I perceived his ball dropping neatly into the car's interior. Arthur himself, brandishing a niblick, was dancing about in the fairway.

"Now what about your moving hazards?" he cried.

At this moment the man in the sweater returned, carrying a spanner. Arthur Jukes sprang towards him.

"I'll give you five pounds to drive me to Royal Square," he said.

I do not know what the sweater-clad young man's engagements for the morning had been originally, but nothing could have been more obliging than the ready way in which he consented to revise them at a moment's notice. I dare say you have noticed that the sturdy peasantry of our beloved land respond to an offer of five pounds as to a bugle-call.

"You're on," said the youth.

"Good!" said Arthur Jukes.

"You think you're darned clever," said Ralph Bingham.

"I know it," said Arthur.

"Well, then," said Ralph, "perhaps you will tell us how you propose to get the ball out of the car when you reach Royal Square?"

"Certainly," replied Arthur. "You will observe on the side of the vehicle a convenient handle which, when turned, opens the door. The door thus opened, I shall chip my ball out!"

"I see," said Ralph. "Yes, I never thought of that."

There was something in the way the man spoke that I did not like. His mildness seemed to me suspicious. He had the air of a man who has something up his sleeve. I was still musing on this when Arthur called to me impatiently to get in. I did so, and we drove off. Arthur was in great spirits. He had ascertained from the young man at the wheel that there was no chance of the opposition being able to hire another car at the garage. This machine was his own property, and the only other one at present in the shop was suffering from complicated trouble of the oiling-system and would not be able to be moved for at least another day.

I, however, shook my head when he pointed out the advantages of his position. I was still wondering about Ralph.

"I don't like it," I said.

"Don't like what?"

"Ralph Bingham's manner."

"Of course not," said Arthur. "Nobody does. There have been complaints on all sides."

"I mean, when you told him how you intended to get the ball out of the car."

"What was the matter with him?"

"He was too—ha!"

"How do you mean he was too—ha?"

"I have it!"

"What?"

"I see the trap he was laying for you. It has just dawned on me. No wonder he didn't object to your opening the door and chipping the ball out. By doing so you would forfeit the match."

"Nonsense! Why?"

"Because," I said, "it is against the rules to tamper with a hazard. If you had got into a sand-bunker, would you smooth away the sand? If you had put your shot under a tree, could your caddie hold up the branches to give you a clear shot? Obviously you would disqualify yourself if you touched that door."

Arthur's jaw dropped.

"What! Then how the deuce am I to get it out?"

"That," I said, gravely, "is a question between you and your Maker."

It was here that Arthur Jukes forfeited the sympathy which I had begun to feel for him. A crafty, sinister look came into his eyes.

"Listen!" he said. "It'll take them an hour to catch up with us. Suppose, during that time, that door happened to open accidentally, as it were, and close again? You wouldn't think it necessary to mention the fact, eh? You would be a good fellow and keep your mouth shut, yes? You might even see your way to go so far as to back me up in a statement to the effect that I hooked it out with my—?"

I was revolted.

"I am a golfer," I said, coldly, "and I obey the rules."

"Yes, but—"

"Those rules were drawn up by—" I bared my head reverently. "By the Committee of the Royal and Ancient at St. Andrews. I have always respected them, and I shall not deviate on this occasion from the policy of a lifetime."

Arthur Jukes relapsed into a moody silence. He broke it once, crossing the West Street Bridge, to observe that he would like to know if I called myself a friend of his—a question which I was able to answer with a whole-hearted negative. After that he did not speak till the car drew up in front of the Majestic Hotel in Royal Square.

Early as the hour was, a certain bustle and animation already prevailed in that centre of the city, and the spectacle of a man in a golf-coat and plus-four knickerbockers hacking with a niblick at the floor of a car was not long in collecting a crowd of some dimensions. Three messenger-boys, four typists, and a gentleman in full evening-dress, who obviously possessed or was friendly with someone who possessed a large cellar, formed the nucleus of it; and they were joined about the time when Arthur addressed the ball in order to play his nine hundred and fifteenth by six news-boys, eleven charladies, and perhaps a dozen assorted loafers, all speculating with the liveliest interest as to which particular asylum had had the honour of sheltering Arthur before he had contrived to elude the vigilance of his custodians.

Arthur had prepared for some such contingency. He suspended his activities with the niblick, and drew from his pocket a large poster, which he proceeded to hang over the side of the car. It read:

COME

TO

MCCLURG AND MACDONALD,

18, WEST STREET,

FOR

ALL GOLFING SUPPLIES.

His knowledge of psychology had not misled him. Directly they gathered that he was advertising something, the crowd declined to look at it; they melted away, and Arthur returned to his work in solitude.

He was taking a well-earned rest after playing his eleven hundred and fifth, a nice niblick shot with lots of wrist behind it, when out of Bridle Street there trickled a weary-looking golf-ball, followed in the order named by Ralph Bingham, resolute but going a trifle at the knees, and Rupert Bailey on a bicycle. The latter, on whose face and limbs the mud had dried, made an arresting spectacle.

"What are you playing?" I inquired.

"Eleven hundred," said Rupert. "We got into a casual dog."

"A casual dog?"

"Yes, just before the bridge. We were coming along nicely, when a stray dog grabbed our nine hundred and ninety-eighth and took it nearly back to Woodfield, and we had to start all over again. How are you getting on?"

"We have just played our eleven hundred and fifth. A nice even game." I looked at Ralph's ball, which was lying close to the kerb. "You are farther from the hole, I think. Your shot, Bingham."

Rupert Bailey suggested breakfast. He was a man who was altogether too fond of creature comforts. He had not the true golfing spirit.

"Breakfast!" I exclaimed.

"Breakfast," said Rupert, firmly. "If you don't know what it is, I can teach you in half a minute. You play it with a pot of coffee, a knife and fork, and about a hundred-weight of scrambled eggs. Try it. It's a pastime that grows on you."

I was surprised when Ralph Bingham supported the suggestion. He was so near holing out that I should have supposed that nothing would have kept him from finishing the match. But he agreed heartily.

"Breakfast," he said, "is an excellent idea. You go along in. I'll follow in a moment. I want to buy a paper."

We went into the hotel, and a few minutes later he joined us. Now that we were actually at the table, I confess that the idea of breakfast was by no means repugnant to me. The keen air and the exercise had given me an appetite, and it was some little time before I was able to assure the waiter definitely that he could cease bringing orders of scrambled eggs. The others having finished also, I suggested a move. I was anxious to get the match over and be free to go home.

We filed out of the hotel, Arthur Jukes leading. When I had passed through the swing-doors, I found him gazing perplexedly up and down the street.

"What is the matter?" I asked.

"It's gone!"

"What has gone?"

"The car!"

"Oh, the car?" said Ralph Bingham. "That's all right. Didn't I tell you about that? I bought it just now and engaged the driver as my chauffeur, I've been meaning to buy a car for a long time. A man ought to have a car."

"Where is it?" said Arthur, blankly. The man seemed dazed.

"I couldn't tell you to a mile or two," replied Ralph. "I told the man to drive to Glasgow. Why? Had you any message for him?"

"But my ball was inside it!"

"Now that," said Ralph, "is really unfortunate! Do you mean to tell me you hadn't managed to get it out yet? Yes, that is a little awkward for you. I'm afraid it means that you lose the match."

"Lose the match?"

"Certainly. The rules are perfectly definite on that point. A period of five minutes is allowed for each stroke. The player who fails to make his stroke within that time loses the hole. Unfortunate, but there it is!"

Arthur Jukes sank down on the path and buried his face in his hands. He had the appearance of a broken man. Once more, I am bound to say, I felt a certain pity for him. He had certainly struggled gamely, and it was hard to be beaten like this on the post.

"Playing eleven hundred and one," said Ralph Bingham, in his odiously self-satisfied voice, as he addressed his ball. He laughed jovially. A messenger-boy had paused close by and was watching the proceedings gravely. Ralph Bingham patted him on the head.

"Well, sonny," he said, "what club would *you* use here?"

"I claim the match!" cried Arthur Jukes, springing up. Ralph Bingham regarded him coldly.

"I beg your pardon?"

"I claim the match!" repeated Arthur Jukes. "The rules say that a player who asks advice from any person other than his caddie shall lose the hole."

"This is absurd!" said Ralph, but I noticed that he had turned pale.

"I appeal to the judges."

"We sustain the appeal," I said, after a brief consultation with Rupert Bailey. "The rule is perfectly clear."

"But you had lost the match already by not playing within five minutes," said Ralph, vehemently.

"It was not my turn to play. You were farther from the pin."

"Well, play now. Go on! Let's see you make your shot."

"There is no necessity," said Arthur, frigidly. "Why should I play when you have already disqualified yourself?"

"I claim a draw!"

"I deny the claim."

"I appeal to the judges."

"Very well. We will leave it to the judges."

I consulted with Rupert Bailey. It seemed to me that Arthur Jukes was entitled to the verdict. Rupert, who, though an amiable and delightful companion, had always been one of Nature's fat-heads, could not see it. We had to go back to our principals and announce that we had been unable to agree.

"This is ridiculous," said Ralph Bingham. "We ought to have had a third judge."

At this moment, who should come out of the hotel but Amanda Trivett! A veritable goddess from the machine.

"It seems to me," I said, "that you would both be well advised to leave the decision to Miss Trivett. You could have no better referee."

"I'm game," said Arthur Jukes.

"Suits me," said Ralph Bingham.

"Why, whatever are you all doing here with your golf clubs?" asked the girl, wonderingly.

"These two gentlemen," I explained, "have been playing a match, and a point has arisen on which the judges do not find themselves in agreement. We need an unbiased outside opinion, and we should like to put it up to you. The facts are as follows: . . ."

Amanda Trivett listened attentively, but, when I had finished, she shook her head.

"I'm afraid I don't know enough about the game to be able to decide a question like that," she said.

"Then we must consult St. Andrews," said Rupert Bailey.

"I'll tell you who might know," said Amanda Trivett, after a moment's thought.

"Who is that?" I asked.

"My fiancé. He has just come back from a golfing holiday. That's why I'm in town this morning. I've been to meet him. He is very good at golf. He won a medal at Little-Mudbury-in-the-Wold the day before he left."

There was a tense silence. I had the delicacy not to look at Ralph or Arthur. Then the silence was broken by a sharp crack. Ralph Bingham had broken his mashie-niblick across his knee. From the direction where Arthur Jukes was standing there came a muffled gulp.

"Shall I ask him?" said Amanda Trivett.

"Don't bother," said Ralph Bingham.

"It doesn't matter," said Arthur Jukes.

CHAPTER 12

IF I WERE A GOLF INSTRUCTOR

JEROME DUNSTAN TRAVERS

If I were a golf instructor it would be some little time before my pupil were allowed to go round the links. Starting with the wooden clubs, driver and brassie, I would have him learn each club separately. I would place him on the tee with a peck of golf balls beside him and a caddie on the fair green ahead to chase them. For an hour at a time I would instruct him in the art of driving alone, striving to correct his mistakes before they became habit, showing him how to grip his club, how to address the ball, how to follow through properly. At the end of an hour, if he were an apt pupil, he would know something about driving whereas, if he had devoted the time to play over the links with six different clubs, he would have learned nothing of value about any one of them.

Then I would take him out on the fair green, place a brassie in his hand and have him put in another hour learning how to use this club. I would explain to him the difference between a good brassie lie and a poor one, laying particular stress upon the fact that a poor lie usually means a poor shot and that one of the first things to learn about this club is when *not* to use it.

If, after an hour of driving and another hour of brassie play, the novice felt the need of something less strenuous, I would then have him devote another hour to putting. I would show him the proper stance and how to grip the club and at the end of his first long lesson he would know more about putting than the average beginner knows after he has played the entire course a dozen times with all the clubs.

If Travers were a golf instructor, he would help a novice with proper stance, amongst other important lessons. *(Tashi-Delek, courtesy of iStock)*

In the same manner I would instruct him in the use of the cleek, mid-iron, and mashie, assigning from half an hour to an hour to each club, and when he had gained a fair working knowledge concerning the manipulation of these clubs and the driver, brassie and putter, I would turn him loose upon the links for an entire round of the eighteen holes. When, in response to different needs, he was compelled to play one club after another, each club would not be a comparative stranger but an old friend with which he was already familiar through hours of practice. I do not carry a cleek myself because I get better results with a driving iron, but I would not advise a novice to follow this example. Also, unlike many players, I do not use a spoon because I found that it shortened my game and that I was playing it when I should have relied upon the mid-iron.

I have laid particular stress upon the necessity for long practice with each club because it is difficult for a beginner to learn the game if he only plays eighteen holes once or twice a week and contents himself with that. Walter J. Travis, who learned to play golf after he was 35, is probably the most remarkable example of what can be accomplished by constant, patient, untiring practice. No man in America ever worked so hard to become a great golfer as he did, and as his reward he has won the amateur championship of the United States three times and the British amateur championship once. Furthermore, he is the only American amateur who ever succeeded in winning the British championship.

When Travis is "off his game" and is not driving, approaching, or putting as he should, he goes out on the links alone and plays with one club or another for hours, practicing the same shot over and over until he has recovered his very best form.

I have done the same thing myself on many occasions. I have played the same shot fifty times. I have putted for two hours at a stretch, placing my ball at varying distances from the hole, trying for short putts, long putts, up hill and down hill putts and putts across a side hill green where the ball must follow a crescent-like course if it is to be holed out or go "dead to the hole." During the afternoon round of my match against Harold H. Hilton, the British champion, at the national amateur championship on the Apawamis links in 1911, I had before me what my own club's champion declared was an "impossible" putt. Of the two thousand people following the match, most of those near the green no doubt shared his opinion. I was not very hopeful myself. My ball was at least twenty feet from the hole, the green was of the undulating, billowy type, and it was a down hill putt.

Remembering the old adage, "Never up, never in," I struck the ball a bit too hard, but it raced down the green as if drawn by a magnet, struck the opposite side of the cup, leaped into the air an inch or two and dropped safely into the hole.

"If you hadn't hit the hole exactly square, Travers, you would have been out of bounds," was Oswald Kirkby's humorous description of the shot after the game.

A putt of this sort is usually called a "lucky" putt, and no doubt there is a certain element of luck about it. Yet hours and hours of practice produced the skill and judgment that sank that "impossible" putt.

When I was playing for the championship at Wheaton in 1912, I got into a very high and formidable bunker on an approach shot. The ball was at the very base of the bunker, close up, and the situation was such a difficult one that I had little hope of getting over with one shot. However, I took my mashie niblick, got well under the ball with it, and much to my gratification the ball crawled up the steep side of the bunker, moved slowly across its top, struck the putting green, and rolled up dead to the hole. A putt gave me a four and captured the hole.

Many a time I have thrown a dozen balls into a bunker and practiced for an hour endeavoring to discover the most successful method of getting out of this difficult hazard. As in the case of the "impossible" putt, the Chicago bunker shot was successful because hours of faithful study had been devoted to learning the way to do it.

Many beginners do a great deal of unnecessary fussing about their clubs, discarding this one or that one as of no value when lack of skill and proper practice are more responsible for bad play than lack of merit in the clubs. A novice should buy good clubs and should be largely guided in their selection by a capable professional or amateur. Clubs with whippy shafts are to be

Many beginners fuss about their clubs, but lack of skill and proper practice tend to be the chief causes of bad play. *(RapidEye, via iStock)*

avoided and the purchase of every new freak club that is placed on the market is a foolish expenditure of money.

In taking up the game the beginner should familiarize himself thoroughly with the etiquette and the rules. Playing the wrong ball, failing to let the pair behind go through when his ball is lost, playing into the pair ahead, or upon the putting green before they have holed out, talking or moving about when an opponent is making a shot, cutting across the course and endeavoring to get in ahead of other players who are going round the entire links—these and other simple infractions of rules and etiquette make the careless beginner unpopular and are the cause of many unpleasant experiences.

Not long ago I heard of a very prominent man who made all sorts of fun of golf and for years refused to try to play. It was a simple, foolish, easy game, he said, and he knew it would not interest him. Finally a friend dragged him to the links, teed a ball for him and told him to drive. When he had struck four times at the ball without even touching it, he became so exasperated that he bought a set of clubs that very day and started with determination to conquer the little white ball.

A month later the friend who had dragged him to the links met him hurrying toward the golf club, although his left arm was in a sling.

"What are you going to do?" asked the friend.

"Oh, I broke my arm," was the enthusiastic reply, "but I'm going down to play with one hand!"

PART THREE

ANECDOTES
FROM THE COURSE

CHAPTER 13

THE GOLF COURSE MYSTERY

CHESTER K. STEELE

There was nothing in that clear, calm day, with its blue sky and its flooding sunshine, to suggest in the slightest degree the awful tragedy so close at hand—that tragedy which so puzzled the authorities and which came so close to wrecking the happiness of several innocent people.

The waters of the inlet sparkled like silver, and over those waters poised the osprey, his rapidly moving wings and fan-spread tail suspending him almost stationary in one spot, while, with eager and far-seeing eyes, he peered into the depths below. The bird was a dark blotch against the perfect blue sky for several seconds, and then, suddenly folding his pinions and closing his tail, he darted downward like a bomb dropped from an aeroplane.

There was a splash in the water, a shower of sparkling drops as the osprey arose, a fish vainly struggling in its talons, and from a dusty gray roadster, which had halted along the highway while the occupant watched the hawk, there came an exclamation of satisfaction.

"Did you see that, Harry?" called the occupant of the gray car to a slightly built, bronzed companion in a machine of vivid yellow, christened by some who had ridden in it the "Spanish Omelet." "Did you see that kill? As clean as a hound's tooth, and not a lost motion of a feather. Some sport—that fishhawk! Gad!"

"Yes, it was a neat bit of work, Gerry. But rather out of keeping with the day."

"Out of keeping? What do you mean?"

"Well, out of tune, if you like that better. It's altogether too perfect a day for a killing of any sort, seems to me."

"Oh, you're getting sentimental all at once, aren't you, Harry?" asked Captain Gerry Poland, with just the trace of a covert sneer in his voice. "I suppose you wouldn't have even a fish-hawk get a much needed meal on a bright, sunshiny day, when, if ever, he must have a whale of an appetite. You'd have him wait until it was dark and gloomy and rainy, with a north-east wind blowing, and all that sort of thing. Now for me, a kill is a kill, no matter what the weather."

"The better the day the worse the deed, I suppose," and Harry Bartlett smiled as he leaned forward preparatory to throwing the switch of his

Harry Bartlett and Captain Gerry Poland watched as the osprey dove into the water and rose with the fish in its talons. *(David Mozzoni, courtesy of iStock)*

machine's self-starter, for both automobiles had come to a stop to watch the osprey.

"Oh, well, I don't know that the day has anything to do with it," said the captain—a courtesy title, bestowed because he was president of the Maraposa Yacht Club. "I was just interested in the clean way the beggar dived after that fish. Flounder, wasn't it?"

"Yes, though usually the birds are glad enough to get a moss-bunker. Well, the fish will soon be a dead one, I suppose."

"Yes, food for the little ospreys, I imagine. Well, it's a good death to die—serving some useful purpose, even if it's only to be eaten. Gad! I didn't expect to get on such a gruesome subject when we started out. By the way, speaking of killings, I expect to make a neat one today on this cup-winners' match."

"How? I didn't know there was much betting."

"Oh, but there is; and I've picked up some tidy odds against our friend Carwell. I'm taking his end, and I think he's going to win."

"Better be careful, Gerry. Golf is an uncertain game, especially when there's a match on among the old boys like Horace Carwell and the crowd of past-performers and cup-winners he trails along with. He's just as likely to pull or slice as the veriest novice, and once he starts to slide he's a goner. No reserve comeback, you know."

"Oh, I've not so sure about that. He'll be all right if he'll let the champagne alone before he starts to play. I'm banking on him. At the same time I haven't bet all my money. I've a ten spot left that says I can beat you to the clubhouse, even if one of my cylinders has been missing the last two miles. How about it?"

"You're on!" said Harry Bartlett shortly.

There was a throb from each machine as the electric motors started the engines, and then they shot down the wide road in clouds of dust—the sinister gray car and the more showy yellow—while above them, driving its talons deeper into the sides of the fish it had caught, the osprey circled off toward its nest of rough sticks in a dead pine tree on the edge of the forest.

And on the white of the flounder appeared bright red spots of blood, some of which dripped to the ground as the cruel talons closed until they met inside.

It was only a little tragedy, such as went on every day in the inlet and adjacent ocean, and yet, somehow, Harry Bartlett, as he drove on with ever-increasing speed in an endeavor to gain a length on his opponent, could not help thinking of it in contrast to the perfect blue of the sky, in which there was not a cloud. Was it prophetic?

Ruddy-faced men, bronze-faced men, pale-faced men; young women, girls, matrons, and "flappers"; caddies burdened with bags of golf clubs and pockets bulging with cunningly found balls; skillful waiters hurrying here and there with trays on which glasses of various shapes, sizes, and of diversified contents tinkled musically—such was the scene at the Maraposa Club on this June morning when Captain Gerry Poland and Harry Bartlett were racing their cars toward it.

It was the chief day of the year for the Maraposa Golf Club, for on it were to be played several matches, not the least in importance being that of the cup-winners, open only to such members as had won prizes in hotly contested contests on the home links.

In spite of the fact that on this day there were to be played several matches, in which visiting and local champions were to try their skill against one another, to the delight of a large gallery, interest centered in the cup-winners' battle. For it was rumored, and not without semblance of truth, that large sums of money would change hands on the result.

Not that it was gambling—oh, my no! In fact any laying of wagers was strictly prohibited by the club's constitution. But there are ways and means of getting cattle through a fence without taking down the bars, and there was talk that Horace Carwell had made a pretty stiff bet with Major Turpin Wardell as to the outcome of the match, the major and Mr. Carwell being rivals of long standing in the matter of drives and putts.

"Beastly fine day, eh, what?" exclaimed Bruce Garrigan, as he set down on a tray a waiter held out to him a glass he had just emptied with every

It was a fine day at the golf course, with not a cloud in sight. *(Arda Guldogan, courtesy of iStock)*

indication of delight in its contents. "If it had been made to order couldn't be improved on," and he flicked from the lapel of Tom Sharwell's Coat some ashes which had blown there from the cigarette which Garrigan had lighted.

"You're right for once, Bruce, old man," was the laughing response. "Never mind the ashes now, you'll make a spot if you rub any harder."

"Right for once? I'm always right!" cried Garrigan. "And it may interest you to know that the total precipitation, including rain and melted snow in Yuma, Arizona, for the calendar year 1917, was three and one tenth inches, being the smallest in the United States."

"It doesn't interest me a bit, Bruce!" laughed Sharwell. "And to prevent you getting any more of those statistics out of your system, come on over and we'll do a little precipitating on our own account. I can stand another Bronx cocktail."

"I'm with you! But, speaking of statistics, did you know that from the national forests of the United States in the last year there was cut 840,-

612,030 board feet of lumber? What the thirty feet were for I don't know, but—"

"And I don't care to know," interrupted Tom. "If you spring any more of those beastly dry figures—say, there comes something that does interest me, though!" he broke in with. "Look at those cars take that turn!"

"Some speed," murmured Garrigan. "It's Bartlett and Poland," he went on, as a shift of wind blew the dust to one side and revealed the gray roadster and the Spanish Omelet. "The rivals are at it again."

Bruce Garrigan, who had a name among the golf club members as a human encyclopaedia, and who, at times, would inform his companions on almost any subject that chanced to come uppermost, tossed away his cigarette and, with Tom Sharwell, watched the oncoming automobile racers.

"They're rivals in more ways than one," remarked Sharwell. "And it looks, now, as though the captain rather had the edge on Harry, in spite of the fast color of Harry's car."

"That's right," admitted Garrigan. "Is it true what I've heard about both of them—that each hopes to place the diamond hoop of proprietorship on the fair Viola?"

"I guess if you've heard that they're both trying for her, it's true enough," answered Sharwell. "And it also happens, if that old lady, Mrs. G. O. S. Sipp, is to be believed, that there, also, the captain has the advantage."

"How's that? I thought Harry had made a tidy sum on that ship-building project he put through."

"He did, but it seems that he and his family have a penchant for doing that sort of thing, and, some years ago, in one of the big mergers in which his family took a prominent part, they, or some one connected with them, pinched the Honorable Horace Carwell so that he squealed for mercy like a lamb led to the Wall street slaughter house."

"So that's the game, is it?"

"Yes. And ever since then, though Viola Carwell has been just as nice to Harry as she has to Gerry—as far as any one can tell—there has been talk that Harry is *persona non grata* as far as her father goes. He never forgives any business beat, I understand."

"Was it anything serious?" asked Garrigan, as they watched the racing automobiles swing around the turn of the road that led to the clubhouse.

"I don't know the particulars. It was before my time—I mean before I paid much attention to business."

"Rot! You don't now. You only think you do. But I'm interested. I expect to have some business dealing with Carwell myself, and if I could get a line————"

"Sorry, but I can't help you out, old man. Better see Harry. He knows the whole story, and he insists that it was all straight on his relatives' part. But it's like shaking a mince pie at a Thanksgiving turkey to mention the matter to Carwell. He hasn't gone so far as to forbid Harry the house, but there's a bit of coldness just the same."

"I see. And that's why the captain has the inside edge on the love game. Well, Miss Carwell has a mind of her own, I fancy."

"Indeed she has! She's more like her mother used to be. I remember Mrs. Carwell when I was a boy. She was a dear, somewhat conventional lady. How she ever came to take up with the sporty Horace, or he with her, was a seven-days' wonder. But they lived happily, I believe."

"Then Mrs. Carwell is dead?"

"Oh, yes—some years. Mr. Carwell's sister, Miss Mary, keeps The Haven up to date for him. You've been there?"

"Once, at a reception. I'm not on the regular calling list, though Miss Viola is pretty enough to—"

"Look out!" suddenly cried Sharwell, as though appealing to the two automobilists, far off as they were. For the yellow car made a sudden swerve and seemed about to turn turtle.

But Bartlett skillfully brought the Spanish Omelet back on the road again, and swung up alongside his rival for the home stretch—the broad highway that ran in front of the clubhouse.

The players who were soon to start out on the links; the guests, the gallery, and the servants gathered to see the finish of the impromptu race, murmurs arising as it was seen how close it was likely to be.

And close it was, for when the two machines, with doleful whinings of brakes, came to a stop in front of the house, the front wheels were in such perfect alignment that there was scarcely an inch of difference.

"A dead heat!" exclaimed Bartlett, as he leaped out and motioned for one of the servants to take the car around to the garage.

"Yes, you win!" agreed Captain Poland, as he pushed his goggles back on his cap. He held out a bill.

"What's it for?" asked Bartlett, drawing back.

"Why, I put up a ten spot that I'd beat you. I didn't, and you win."

"Buy drinks with your money!" laughed Bartlett. "The race was to be for a finish, not a dead heat We'll try it again, sometime."

"All right—any time you like!" said the captain crisply, as he sat down at a table after greeting some friends. "But you won't refuse to split a quart with me?"

"No. My throat is as dusty as a vacuum cleaner. Have any of the matches started yet, Bruce?" he asked, turning to the Human Encyclopædia.

"Only some of the novices. And, speaking of novices, do you know that in Scotland there are fourteen thousand, seven hundred—"

"Cut it, Bruce! Cut it!" begged the captain. "Sit in—you and Tom—and we'll make it two bottles. Anything to choke off your flow of useless statistics!" and he laughed good-naturedly.

"When does the cup-winners' match start?" asked Bartlett, as the four young men sat about the table under the veranda. "That's the one I'm interested in."

"In about an hour," announced Sharwell, as he consulted a card. "Hardly any of the veterans are here yet."

"Has Mr. Carwell arrived?" asked Captain Poland, as he raised his glass and seemed to be studying the bubbles that spiraled upward from the hollow stem.

"You'll know when he gets here," answered Bruce Garrigan.

"How so?" asked the captain. "Does he have an official announcer?"

"No, but you'll hear his car before you see it."

"New horn?"

"No, new car—new color—new everything!" said Garrigan. "He's just bought a new ten thousand dollar French car, and it's painted red, white, and blue, and . . ."

"Red, white, and blue?" chorused the other three men.

"Yes. Very patriotic. His friends don't know whether he's honoring Uncle Sam or the French Republic. However, it's all the same. His car is a wonder."

"I must have a brush with him!" murmured Captain Poland.

"Don't. You'll lose out," advised Garrigan. "It can do eighty on fourth speed, and Carwell is sporty enough to slip it into that gear if he needed to."

"Um! Guess I'll wait until I get my new machine, then," decided the captain.

There was more talk, but Bartlett gradually dropped out of the conversation and went to walk about the club grounds.

Maraposa was a social, as well as a golfing, club, and the scene of many dances and other affairs. It lay a few miles back from the shore near Lakeside, in New Jersey. The clubhouse was large and elaborate, and the grounds around it were spacious and well laid out.

Not far away was Loch Harbor, where the yachts of the club of which Captain Gerry Poland was president anchored, and a mile or so in the opposite direction was Lake Tacoma, on the shore of which was Lakeside. A rather exclusive colony summered there, the hotel numbering many wealthy persons among its patrons.

Harry Bartlett, rather wishing he had gone in for golf more devotedly, was wandering about, casually greeting friends and acquaintances, when he heard his name called from the cool and shady depths of a summer-house on the edge of the golf links.

"Oh, Minnie! How are you?" he cordially greeted a rather tall and dark girl who extended her slim hand to him. "I didn't expect to see you today."

"Oh, I take in all the big matches, though I don't play much myself," answered Minnie Webb. "I'm surprised to find you without a caddy, though, Harry."

"Too lazy, I'm afraid. I'm going to join the gallery today. Meanwhile, if you don't mind, I'll sit in here and help you keep cool."

"It isn't very hard to do that today," and she moved over to make room for him. "Isn't it just perfect weather!"

At one time Minnie Webb and Harry Bartlett had been very close friends—engaged, some rumors had it. But now they were jolly good companions, that was all.

"Seen the Carwells' new machine?" asked Bartlett.

"No, but I've heard about it. I presume they'll drive up in it today."

"Does Viola run it?"

"I haven't heard. It's a powerful machine, someone said—more of a racer than a touring car, Mr. Blossom was remarking."

"Well, he ought to know. I understand he's soon to be taken into partnership with Mr. Carwell."

"I don't know," murmured Minnie, and she seemed suddenly very much interested in the vein structure of a leaf she pulled from a vine that covered the summerhouse.

Bartlett smiled. Gossip had it that Minnie Webb and LeGrand Blossom, Mr. Carwell's private secretary, were engaged. But there had been no formal announcement, though the two had been seen together more frequently of late than mere friendship would warrant.

There was a stir in front of the clubhouse, followed by a murmur of voices, and Minnie, peering through a space in the vines, announced:

"There's the big car now. Oh, I don't like that color at all! I'm as patriotic as any one, but to daub a perfectly good car up like that—well, it's—"

"Sporty, I suppose Carwell thinks," finished Bartlett. He had risen as though to leave the summerhouse, but as he saw Captain Poland step up and offer his hand to Viola Carwell, he drew back and again sat down beside Minnie.

A group gathered about the big French car, obviously to the delight of Mr. Carwell, who was proud of the furor created by his latest purchase.

Though he kept up his talk with Minnie in the summer-house, Harry Bartlett's attention was very plainly not on his present companion nor the conversation. At any other time Minnie Webb would have noticed it and taxed him with it, but now, she, too, had her attention centered elsewhere. She watched eagerly the group about the big machine, and her eyes followed the figure of a man who descended from the rear seat and made his way out along a path that led to a quiet spot.

"I think I'll go in now," murmured Minnie Webb. "I have to see—"

Bartlett was not listening. In fact he was glad of the diversion, for he saw Viola Carwell turn with what he thought was impatience aside from Captain Poland, and that was the very chance the other young man had been waiting for.

He followed Minnie Webb from the little pavilion, paying no attention to where she drifted. But he made his way through the press of persons to where Viola stood, and he saw her eyes light up as he approached. His, too, seemed brighter.

"I was wondering if you would come to see dad win," she murmured to him, as he took her hand, and Captain Poland, with a little bow, stepped back.

"You knew I'd come, didn't you?" Bartlett asked in a low voice.

"I hoped so," she murmured. "Now, Harry," she went on in a low voice, as they moved aside, "this will be a good time for you to smooth things over with father. If he wins, as he feels sure he will, you must congratulate him very heartily—exceptionally so. Make a fuss over him, so to speak. He'll be club champion, and it will seem natural for you to bubble over about it."

"But why should I, Viola? I haven't done anything to merit his displeasure."

"I know. But you remember what a touch-fire he is. He's always held that business matter against you, though I'm sure you had nothing to do with it. Now, if he wins, and I hope he will, you can take advantage of it to get on better terms with him, and—"

"Well, I'm willing to be friends, you know that, Viola. But I can't pretend—I never could!"

"You're stubborn, Harry!" and Viola pouted.

"Well, perhaps I am. When I know I'm right."

"Couldn't you forget it just once?"

"I don't see how!"

"Oh, you provoke me! But if you won't you won't, I suppose. Only it would be such a good chance—"

"Well, I'll see him after the match, Viola. I'll do my best to be decent."

"You must go a little farther than that, Harry. Dad will be all worked up if he wins, and he'll want a fuss made over him. It will be the very chance for you."

"All right—I'll do my best," murmured Bartlett. And then a servant came up to summon him to the telephone.

Viola was not left long alone, for Captain Poland was watching her from the tail of his eye, and he was at her side before Harry Bartlett was out of sight.

"Perhaps you'd like to come for a little spin with me, Miss Carwell," said the captain. "I just heard that they've postponed the cup-winners' match an hour; and unless you want to sit around here—"

"Come on!" cried Viola, impulsively. "It's too perfect a day to sit around, and I'm only interested in my father's match."

There was another reason why Viola Carwell was glad of the chance to go riding with Captain Poland just then. She really was a little provoked with Bartlett's stubbornness, or what she called that, and she thought it might "wake him up," as she termed it, to see her with the only man who might be classed as his rival.

As for herself, Viola was not sure whether or not she would admit Captain Poland to that class. There was time enough yet.

And so, as Bartlett went in to the telephone, to answer a call that had come most inopportunely for him, Viola Carwell and Captain Poland swept off along the pleasantly shaded country road.

Left to herself, for which just then she was thankful, Minnie Webb drifted around until she met LeGrand Blossom.

"What's the matter, Lee?" she asked him in a low voice, and he smiled with his eyes at her, though his face showed no great amount of jollity. "You're as solemn as though every railroad stock listed had dropped ten points just after you bought it."

"No, it isn't quite as bad as that," he said, as he fell into step beside her, and they strolled off on one of the less-frequented walks.

"I thought everything was going so well with you. Has there been any hitch in the partnership arrangement?" asked Minnie.

"No, not exactly."

"Have you lost money?"

"No, I can't say that I have."

"Then for goodness' sake what is it? Do I have to pump you like a newspaper reporter?" and Minnie Webb laughed, showing a perfect set of teeth that contrasted well against the dark red and tan of her cheeks.

"Oh, I don't know that it's anything much," replied LeGrand Blossom.

"It's *something!*" insisted Minnie.

"Well, yes, it is. And as it'll come out, sooner or later, I might as well tell you now," he said, with rather an air of desperation, and as though driven to it "Have you heard any rumors that Mr. Carwell is in financial difficulties?"

"Why, no! The idea! I always thought he had plenty of money. Not a multi-millionaire, of course, but better off financially than any one else in Lakeside."

"He was once; but he won't be soon, if he keeps up the pace he's set of late," went on LeGrand Blossom, and his voice was gloomy.

"What do you mean?"

"Well, things don't look so well as they did. He was very foolish to buy that ten-thousand-dollar yacht so soon after spending even more than that on this red, white, and blue monstrosity of his!"

"You don't mean to tell me he's bought a yacht, too?"

"Yes, the *Osprey* that Colonel Blakeson used to sport up and down the coast in. Paid a cool ten thousand for it, though if he had left it to me I could have got it for eight, I'm sure."

"Well, twenty thousand dollars oughtn't to worry Mr. Carwell, I should think," returned Minnie.

"It wouldn't have, a year ago," answered LeGrand. "But he's been on the wrong side of the market for some time. Then, too, something new has cropped up about that old Bartlett deal."

"You mean the one over which Harry's uncle and Mr. Carwell had such a fuss?"

"Yes. Mr. Carwell's never got over that. And there are rumors that he lost quite a sum in a business transaction with Captain Poland."

"Oh, dear!" sighed the girl. "Isn't business horrid! I'm glad I'm not a man. But what is this about Captain Poland?"

"I don't know—haven't heard it all yet, as Mr. Carwell doesn't tell me everything, even if he has planned to take me into partnership with him. But now I'm not so keen on it."

"Keen on what, Lee?" and Minnie Webb leaned just the least bit nearer to his side.

"On going into partnership with a man who spends money so lavishly when he needs all the ready cash he can lay his hands on. But don't mention this to any one, Minnie. If it got out it might precipitate matters, and then the whole business would tumble down like a house of cards. As it is, I may be able to pull him out But I've put the soft pedal on the partnership talk."

"Has Mr. Carwell mentioned it of late?"

"No. All he seems to be interested in is this golf game that may make him club champion. But keep secret what I have told you."

Minnie Webb nodded assent, and they turned back toward the clubhouse, for they had reached a too secluded part of the grounds.

Meanwhile, Viola Carwell was not enjoying her ride with Captain Poland as much as she had expected she would. As a matter of fact it had been undertaken largely to cause Bartlett a little uneasiness; and as the car spun on she paid less and less attention to the captain.

Seeing this, the latter changed his mind concerning something he had fully expected to speak to Viola about that day, if he got the chance.

Captain Poland was genuinely in love with Viola, and he had reason to feel that she cared for him, though whether enough to warrant a declaration of love on his part was hard to understand.

"But I won't take a chance now," mused the captain, rather moodily; and the talk descended to mere monosyllables on the part of both of them. "I must see Carwell and have it out with him about that insurance deal. Maybe he holds that against me, though the last time I talked with him he gave me to understand that I'd stand a better show than Harry. I must see him after the game. If he wins he'll be in a mellow humor, particularly after a bottle or so. That's what I'll do."

The captain spun his car up in front of the clubhouse and helped Viola out.

"I think we are in plenty of time for your father's match," he remarked.

"Yes," she assented. "I don't see any of the veterans on the field yet," and she looked across the perfect course. "I'll go to look for dad and wish him luck. He always wants me to do that before he starts his medal play. See you again, Captain;" and with a friendly nod she left the somewhat chagrined yachtsman.

When Captain Poland had parked his car he took a short cut along a path that led through a little clump of bushes. Midway he heard voices. In an instant he recognized them as those of Horace Carwell and Harry Bartlett. He heard Bartlett say:

"But don't you see how much better it would be to drop it all—to have nothing more to do with her?"

"Look here, young man, you mind your own business!" snapped Mr. Carwell. "I know what I'm doing!"

"I haven't any doubt of it, Mr. Carwell; but I ventured to suggest," went on Bartlett.

"Keep your suggestions to yourself, if you please. I've had about all I want from you and your family. And if I hear any more of your impudent talk—"

Then Captain Poland moved away, for he did not want to hear any more.

In the meantime Viola hurried back to the clubhouse, and forced herself to be gay. But, somehow, a cloud seemed to have come over her day.

The throng had increased, and she caught sight, among the press, of Jean Forette, their chauffeur.

"Have you seen my father since he arrived, Jean?" asked Viola.

"Oh, he is somewhere about, I suppose," was the answer, and it was given in such a surly tone and with such a churlish manner that Viola flushed with anger and bit her lips to keep back a sharp retort.

At that moment Minnie Webb strolled past. She had heard the question and the answer.

"I just saw your father going out with the other contestants, Viola," said Minnie Webb, for they were friends of some years' standing. "I think they are going to start to play. I wonder why they say the French are such a polite race?" she went on, speaking lightly to cover Viola's confusion caused by the chauffeur's manner. "He was positively insulting."

"He was," agreed Viola. "But I shouldn't mind him, I suppose. He does not like the new machine, and father has told him to find another place by the end of the month. I suppose that has piqued him."

While there were many matches to be played at the Maraposa Club that day, interest, as far as the older members and their friends were concerned, was centered in that for cup-winners. These constituted the best players—the veterans of the game—and the contest was sure to be interesting and close.

Horace Carwell was a "sport," in every meaning of the term. Though a man well along in his forties, he was as lithe and active as one ten years younger. He motored, fished, played golf, hunted, and of late had added yachting to his amusements. He was wealthy, as his father had been before him, and owned a fine home in New York, but he spent a large part of every year at Lakeside, where he might enjoy the two sports he loved best—golfing and yachting.

Viola was an only child, her mother having died when she was about sixteen, and since then Mr. Carwell's maiden sister had kept watch and ward over the handsome home, The Haven. Viola, though loving her father with the natural affection of a daughter and some of the love she had lavished on her mother, was not altogether in sympathy with the sporting proclivities of Mr. Carwell.

True, she accompanied him to his golf games and sailed with him or rode in his big car almost as often as he asked her. And she thoroughly enjoyed these things. But what she did not enjoy was the rather too jovial comradeship that followed on the part of the men and women her father associated with. He was a good liver and a good spender, and he liked to have about him such persons—men "sleek and fat," who if they did not "sleep o' nights," at least had the happy faculty of turning night into day for their own amusement.

So, in a measure, Viola and her father were out of sympathy, as had been husband and wife before her; though there had never been a whisper of real incompatibility; nor was there now, between father and daughter.

"Fore!"

It was the warning cry from the first tee to clear the course for the start of the cup-winners' match. In anticipation of some remarkable playing, an unusually large gallery would follow the contestants around. The best caddies had been selected, clubs had been looked to with care and tested, new balls were got out, and there was much subdued excitement, as befitted the occasion.

Mr. Carwell, his always-flushed face perhaps a trifle more like a mild sunset than ever, strolled to the first tee. He swung his driver with freedom and ease to make sure it was the one that best suited him, and then turned to Major Wardell, his chief rival.

"Do you want to take any more?" he asked meaningly.

"No, thank you," was the laughing response. "I've got all I can carry. Not that I'm going to let you beat me, but I'm always a stroke or two off in my play when the sun's too bright, as it is now. However, I'm not crawling."

"You'd better not!" declared his rival. "As for me, the brighter the sun the better I like it. Well, are we all ready?"

The officials held a last consultation and announced that play might start. Mr. Carwell was to lead.

The first hole was not the longest in the course, but to place one's ball on fair ground meant driving very surely, and for a longer distance than most players liked to think about. Also a short distance from the tee was a deep ravine, and unless one cleared that it was a handicap hard to overcome.

Mr. Carwell made his little tee of sand with care, and placed the ball on the apex. Then he took his place and glanced back for a moment to where Viola stood between Captain Poland and Harry Bartlett. Something like a little frown gathered on the face of Horace Carwell as he noted the presence of Bartlett, but it passed almost at once.

"Well, here goes, ladies and gentlemen!" exclaimed Mr. Carwell in rather loud tones and with a free and easy manner he did not often assume. "Here's where I bring home the bacon and make my friend, the major, eat humble pie."

Viola flushed. It was not like her father to thus boast. On the contrary he was usually what the Scotch call a "canny" player. He never predicted that he was going to win, except, perhaps, to his close friends. But he was now boasting like the veriest schoolboy.

"Here I go!" he exclaimed again, and then he swung at the ball with his well-known skill.

It was a marvelous drive, and the murmurs of approbation that greeted it seemed to please Mr. Carwell.

"Let's see anybody beat that!" he cried as he stepped off the tee to give place to Major Wardell.

Mr. Carwell's white ball had sailed well up on the putting green of the first hole, a shot seldom made at Maraposa.

"A few more strokes like that and he'll win the match," murmured Bartlett.

"And when he does, don't forget what I told you," whispered Viola to him.

He found her hand, hidden at her side in the folds of her dress, and pressed it. She smiled up at him, and then they watched the major swing at his ball.

"It's going to be a corking match," murmured more than one member of the gallery, as they followed the players down the field.

"If any one asked me, I should say that Carwell had taken just a little too much champagne to make his strokes true toward the last hole," said Tom Sharwell to Bruce Garrigan.

"Perhaps," was the admission. "But I'd like to see him win. And, for the sake of saying something, let me inform you that in Africa last year there were used in nose rings alone for the natives seventeen thousand four hundred and twenty-one pounds of copper wire. While for anklets—"

"I'll buy you a drink if you chop it off short!" offered Sharwell.

"Taken!" exclaimed Garrigan, with a grin.

The cup play went on, the four contestants being well matched, and the shots duly applauded from hole to hole.

The turn was made and the homeward course began, with the excitement increasing as it was seen that there would be the closest possible finish, between the major and Mr. Carwell at least.

"What's the row over there?" asked Bartlett suddenly, as he walked along with Viola and Captain Poland.

"Where?" inquired the captain.

"Among those autos. Looks as if one was on fire."

"It does," agreed Viola. "But I can see our patriotic palfrey, so I guess it's all right. There are enough people over there, anyhow. But it is something!"

There was a dense cloud of smoke hovering over the place where some of the many automobiles were parked at one corner of the course. Still it might be some one starting his machine, with too much oil being burned in the cylinders.

"Now for the last hole!" exulted Mr. Carwell, as they approached the eighteenth. "I've got you two strokes now, Major, and I'll have you four by the end of the match."

"I'm not so sure of that," was the laughing and good-natured reply.

There was silence in the gallery while the players made ready for the last hole.

There was a sharp impact as Mr. Carwell's driver struck the little white ball and sent it sailing in a graceful curve well toward the last hole.

"A marvelous shot!" exclaimed Captain Poland. "On the green again! Another like that and he'll win the game!"

"And I can do it, too!" boasted Carwell, who overheard what was said.

The others drove off in turn, and the play reached the final stage of putting. Viola turned as though to go over and see what the trouble was among the automobiles. She looked back as she saw her father stoop to send the ball into the little depressed cup. She felt sure that he would win, for she had kept a record of his strokes and those of his opponents. The game was all but over.

"I wonder if there can be anything the matter with our car?" mused Viola, as she saw the smoke growing denser. "Dad's won, so I'm going over to see. Perhaps that chauffeur—"

She did not finish the sentence. She turned to look back at her father once more, and saw him make the putt that won the game at the last hole. Then, to her horror she saw him reel, throw up his hands, and fall heavily in a heap, while startled cries reached her ears.

"Oh! Oh! What has happened?" she exclaimed, and deadly fear clutched at her heart—and not without good cause.

CHAPTER 14

PLAYING PINE VALLEY— AN OUT-OF-BODY EXPERIENCE

JOHN SABINO

A dear friend who shot 78 the first time he played Royal Melbourne's West course gave me a wooden board that lists top golf courses. I hung the board in my office at work and it was a natural conversation piece. It completely changes the dynamic of having to be a golf whore. People look at it and ask what it is; most think it's neat and scan down the list of courses. Typically, they will say, "Oh, I know a member at Oakland Hills, I should introduce you." My experience is you do not have to ask with the peg board up, people volunteer to help. The boards are sold through Golf Links to the Past, located in Pebble Beach, and are available for sale on their website.

One of the ultimate coups in my quest was the way I played the number one ranked course in the world, which I am fortunate to live an hour from. One day I was sitting in my office and a colleague came in and we started talking. He had been in my office countless times before and had seen my peg board but never said anything. In an utter act of goodwill and kindness, he said out of the blue, "Hey John, we should go out and play Pine Valley; are you interested?" I didn't even know he was a member.

I was speechless for a good thirty seconds as it registered. When I told him yes, he said, "Great, how does Sunday look?" Putting aside that I would have to skip going to church, my son's soccer game, and my wedding anniversary (just kidding on the last point, but that would be a tough call), I said, "Sunday looks

Pine Valley, New Jersey, a stand-alone golf course and township. *(John Sabino)*

open," to which he replied, "As long as the weather holds up, let's do it." For the next five days I checked the weather online every half hour. One of my friends who was jealous I was playing was hoping there would be a nor'easter on the appointed day, but the weather was ideal—a crisp fall day with a temperature of seventy-three degrees and low humidity. The Weather Channel's "golf index" indicator tells the whole story, it was: "10 out of 10 (Excellent)."

On the morning of my round, I put on my finest dress slacks and best golf shirt; no fraying khakis at Pine Valley. I prepared my car, filled it with gas, and checked the tire pressure, the oil, and the wiper fluid. If you haven't figured it out, I'm a little compulsive, but nothing was going to stop me from having a flawless day. I drove down the New Jersey Turnpike at fifty-five miles per hour, which is difficult to do since the average car and truck is going over seventy miles per hour. I was a little-old-lady out for my Sunday drive. I did not need to be pulled over by a state trooper on my way to Pine Valley so I was taking no chances at all. I also brought plenty of cash, because the pro shop didn't take credit cards at the time (it does now) and I wanted to buy a large quantity of logoed merchandise.

New Jersey is a most unusual state in many ways, especially when it comes to something called local-rule. Even though it is one of the smallest states, it has over 550 separate municipalities or governing bodies. Aside from being a revered golf course, Pine Valley is its own stand-alone municipality, which consists of only the golf course and a few houses owned by members. Under New Jersey law every municipality has to have a town hall, a school district, et cetera, in order to be able to govern itself. Pine Valley has each of these and its own stand-alone police force as well. It is set up this way so it can keep complete control over its affairs without anybody poking into its business.

Pine Valley's location—similar to the presidential retreat at Camp David—isn't exactly unknown, you just have go out of your way to find it. Located in an ordinary middle-class New Jersey suburb, the area surrounding the course is not grand and does not hint at the greatness that exists behind the fence separating this unrivaled place from the rest of the world. To get to Pine Valley you drive to the tiny Clementon Amusement Park, which saw its best days long ago but still functions seasonally. Behind the amusement park, down a two-lane road, on the other side of a set of railroad tracks is the Pine Valley Administration building. This Lilliputian building contains the entire infrastructure for the town of Pine Valley, population twenty, which includes the municipal court, police headquarters, and town hall.

I drove over the railroad tracks, through the fence, and approached the guardhouse. My name was on the clipboard, I had no food sticking out of my teeth, and my fly was zipped, so I was waved in. I had reread *Zen Golf* in anticipation of playing and tried to settle myself down a little because it is such a peerless place: remember to breathe, meditate, and enter the zone. The clubhouse is modest and understated and has few trappings, because it is about golf only. It would do the officials at the USGA and PGA a world of good to visit Pine Valley every so often as a refresher in what makes golf great.

It is not about having high rough or lots of water, it is about the strategic nature of the course and having to use your head to play well.

The course is, no doubt about it, one of the best in the world, and the club and the township an exclusive enclave. When playing at Pine Valley you are away from the world and communing with nature. The routing of the course is the best in the world; it is so diverse and well thought-out. To give you a sense of how much attention they pay to course conditioning, after they cut the fairways, they take a rope and pull it across them to remove excess clippings so they are pristine. The sandy waste areas off the fairway are to be avoided because they are true hazards. There are no rakes in any of the sand and being in them is a quick way to run up a big number. It is certainly one of the most visually intimidating courses in the world. Every tee shot requires a forced carry over the menacing sandy waste areas. Unwavering pinpoint accuracy is required to score well at Pine Valley. If you are long and accurate off the

Pine Valley, 9th hole. *(John Sabino)*

tee, the fairways are lush and generous, setting you up to score well; if you have the misfortune of slicing or pulling your tee shot, or—heaven forbid—hitting it short of the fairways, Pine Valley will torture you. Assuming you hit the fairways, the key to scoring is holding the perfectly conditioned and lightning fast greens (easier said than done) and having a deft touch while putting.

We stopped for lunch after our morning round and then played again. The entire experience had an out-of-body feeling for me and luckily I played a bit better than my handicap. By the end of the day I was never more physically and mentally drained in all my life. After I drove home I opened a bottle of Irish whiskey I had been saving for a special occasion, a twenty-five-year-old Bushmills Millennium Malt, bottled in the year 2000, and sipped it neat, accompanied by a Bolivar No. 2. I passed out on my back deck a happy man. Although I travel frequently and pride myself on being home so I can attend all my kids' sporting events, I had to make an exception and missed my son's game, which he has forgiven me for.

As an illustration of how revered Pine Valley is in the world of golf, consider the story Jack Nicklaus tells in his biography *My Story*. He was on his honeymoon and driving from New York to Atlantic City, which isn't far from the course. He arrived at the course unannounced and asked if he could play. They accommodated him but at the time Pine Valley didn't allow women on the property, so his wife, Barbara, stayed outside the fence, driving around, trying to spy him occasionally around the perimeter.

Pine Valley is the true north of a pure golfing experience and every golfer should try to visit at least once, even if you can't play the course. Each September the club hosts the Crump Cup, their club championship and a private tournament, and they allow spectators to come and watch on the final Sunday. After parking at the nearby amusement park, yellow buses—wholly appropriate because you feel like a child who is agog on your way to the first day of school—shuttle you over to the course. Spectators are allowed unrestricted access (for a twenty-dollar parking fee) to the grounds without any ropes up, although you are not allowed in the pro shop or clubhouse. It is worth attending so you can see the property and the impressive routing.

CHAPTER 15

THE STORY OF THE HONG-KONG MEDAL

W. G. VAN T. SUTPHEN

At the age of thirty-five but one illusion remained to Henry Alderson, rich, single, and a member in good and regular standing of the Marion County Golf Club. It is hardly necessary to add that it was only in his capacity as a golfer that he lived again in the rose-colored atmosphere of youth, for after the third decade there is no other possible form of self-deception. And it is equally superfluous to remark that he was a very poor golfer, for it is only the duffers at the royal and ancient game who have any leisure for the exercise of the imagination; the medal-winners are obliged to confine their attention to hitting the ball clean and to keeping their eye in for short putts. It was for Henry Alderson and his kind to keep trade brisk for the ball and club makers, and to win phenomenal matches against the redoubtable *Col. Bogey*—a game which may be magnificent, but which is certainly not golf. Still, the diversion was unquestionably a harmless one, and served to keep him in the open air and from an overclose application to business. Moreover, it was absolutely certain that the secret of success lay well within his grasp. A few more days of practice, the final acquisition of that peculiar turn of the wrist, and then!—Henry Alderson took a fresh grip on the familiar lofting-iron that had deceived him so often, and topped another ball along the turf. Of course the delusion was a hopeless one, but he was happy in its possession;

and if we who look on have become wiser in our day and generation—why, so much the worse for us.

It was a bright autumn morning, and Henry Alderson stood at the tee looking at the little red flag that marked the location of the tenth hole, two hundred and thirty yards away. He had done fairly well on the outgoing course, but this hole had always been a stumbling-block to him, and that dreadful double hazard, a scant hundred yards down the course, looked particularly savage on this particular morning. On the left lurked an enormous sand-pit, which was popularly known as the "Devil"; and the "Deep Sea," in the shape of an ice pond, was only a few yards to the right. Straight between them lay the path to glory, but for a "slice" or a "foozle" there remained only destruction and double figures.

Henry Alderson shuddered as he looked, and incontinently forgot all about "slow back." Crack! and the "gutty" had disappeared beneath the treacherous waters of the "Deep Sea." With painful deliberation he teed another ball and mentally added two to his score. The club-head swung back,

On the left lurked a sand-pit known as the "Devil." *(mauinow1, courtesy of iStock)*

and for one fatal instant his eye wandered from the ball. Bang! and it had gone to the "Devil." Without a word Mr. Alderson took his expensive collection of seventeen clubs from the hands of his caddie and descended into the bunker to meet the Evil One.

It was just fifteen minutes after eleven when Henry Alderson entered upon his ghostly conflict with all the Powers of Darkness. At twenty minutes of twelve the caddie, tired of inaction, crept cautiously to the edge of the bunker and looked in. His master held in his hand a costly patented "driver" that was alleged to be unbreakable. Placing one foot upon the head of the club, he kicked judiciously but with determination at the precise place where the "scare " is whipped to the shaft, and then carefully added the fragments to the heap of broken putters, cleeks, and brasseys that lay before him. The boy, who was wise in his generation, waited for no more, but fled to the club-house.

Henry Alderson came up out of the bunker, took half a dozen new balls from the pocket of his red coat, and deliberately flung them into the "Deep Sea." He then tore his score-card into bits, divested himself of cap and shoes, laid his watch and purse where they would be readily observed, and walked with a firm step to the border of the pond.

Suddenly a quickly moving shadow projected itself over his shoulder, and a cheerful, albeit an unfamiliar, voice hailed him. He turned and saw a stranger standing close beside him. The new-comer was an odd-looking personage, dressed in a semiclerical suit of rusty black, and carrying an old cotton umbrella and a well-stuffed carpet-bag. He had a keen-looking, smooth-shaven face, with piercing black eyes and an aggressive nose. His complexion was of a curious pallor, as though untouched by wind or sun, but there was nothing in his appearance to indicate either ill-health or decrepitude.

"Possibly a colporteur," thought Henry Alderson. "At any rate, he's no golfer."

"How are you making out?" inquired the stranger, in a tone of polite interest.

It was on the tip of Henry Alderson's tongue to answer, "Fifty-five for nine holes " (his actual score being sixty-three), but at this awful moment, when all the solid realities of life were crumbling away beneath his feet, the lie seemed so small, so pitiful, so mean, and he replied, "Came out in forty-two, but then I lost a shot through having my ball lifted by a dog."

The stranger did not seem to be visibly impressed. "Pooh!" he said, airily; "I should hardly call that golf."

"Perhaps you play yourself," returned Alderson, with what he considered to be a sarcastic inflection.

"Not as a general thing, though I do a round or so occasionally," said the dark gentleman, placidly. Then opening his carpet-bag and taking out a golf ball, "It's a very pretty drive from where we stand. If you will allow me."

He teed the ball, and, with what seemed to be an almost contemptuous disregard of all rules for correct driving, swung against it the crook handle of his old cotton umbrella. Crack! and it went away like a rifle-bullet, close to the ground for one hundred and twenty yards, and then, towering upward in the manner of a rocketing pigeon, caught the full strength of the breeze for a hundred yards of further carry, and dropped dead on the putting-green. Henry Alderson gasped.

"Shall we walk on?" said the stranger. It was a long putt on the green, but the umbrella was again equal to the occasion. Henry Alderson's eyes sparkled. This was an umbrella worth having.

"It makes no difference what kind of a club you use," said the gentleman in black, apparently reading his thoughts. "But with this particular make of ball you can accomplish any shot at will, no matter how difficult."

"I'd like to try that kind of ball," said Alderson, eagerly. "Can you give me the maker's address?"

"If you will accept this one, it is entirely at your service."

Henry Alderson stretched out his hand, and then as quickly withdrew it. He remembered now that when the obliging stranger had opened his bag it had appeared to be filled with what looked like legal papers—contracts perhaps—and there was a dreadful significance in the fact that all the signatures were in red. Of course it might have been carmine ink, and probably was, but it looked suspicious.

"If it's a question of signing my name to anything," he faltered, "I don't think that I can accept. I've made it a rule—er—never to go upon anybody's paper. It's—er—business, you know."

The stranger smiled indulgently. "You are quite right. Nevertheless, you need have no scruples about accepting my gift, for there is no obligation of any kind involved in the transaction."

Henry Alderson trembled, and looked furtively at the dark gentleman's feet, which, as he now observed, were encased in a pair of arctic galoshes some four sizes too large. Clearly there was no definite information to be gained in that quarter; and as the field that they were in was used as a pasture for cattle, the presence of hoof-marks could mean nothing either way. There was nothing to do but to chance it, and he was not long in making up his mind. He took the ball and stowed it away in his pocket.

The stranger nodded approvingly. "I think that I may congratulate you in advance upon your success in winning the club handicap this afternoon."

"But suppose that I lose the ball?" said Alderson, with a sudden accession of doubtfulness.

"Impossible. If your caddie has been negligent, you have only to whistle, and the ball will keep on answering ' Here ' until you come up with it. And, moreover, it is indestructible."

"It makes no difference what club I use?"

"None whatever. If you care to, you can drive that ball two hundred yards with a feather bolster."

"I shall endeavor to do so," laughed Alderson. "You won't—er—come and have a bite of luncheon with me?"

"Not today," said the stranger, politely. "But we shall probably meet again. Good luck to you, and may your success end only with the winning of the Hong-Kong Medal."

The two men bowed, and the dark gentleman walked off. He went to the edge of the "Devil" sand-bunker, marched straight into it, and disappeared.

Moved by a sudden impulse, Henry Alderson followed and looked in. There was nothing to be seen, but he thought that he could detect a slight trace of sulphur in the air. However, one may be easily deceived in such matters.

As Henry Alderson trudged back to the club-house it seemed as though the events of the last half-hour had been nothing more than the disordered fancies of a noon-day nightmare. But there was the ball in his hand, the tangible evidence of what had happened. And, after all, the bargain had been entirely in his favor. Whoever the dark gentleman may have been, and Henry Alderson shuddered as he reflected upon one unholy possibility, he was certainly no business man. The wonderful ball was in his, Henry Alderson's, possession, and his chances of eternal salvation were as good as ever.

"Somebody has been stupid," chuckled Mr. Alderson to himself as he entered the grill-room of the club and took up the luncheon card.

The handicap match had been put down for three o'clock. It was a monthly affair, and the winner had the proud distinction of wearing a silver cross for the following period of thirty days. It was a coveted honor, but of course not to be compared with the Hong-Kong Medal, which was always played for at the end of the golfing year. No one knew why it was called the Hong-Kong Medal, and it was certain that its donor had never in his life been out of the Middle States. But the appellation seemed to chime in with the somewhat fanciful phraseology that prevails in all things pertaining to golf, and it possessed a sonorous clang tint that was suggestive of tomtoms and barbaric victories.

It is needless to say that Henry Alderson invariably entered all the club competitions, and as invariably came out at the bottom of the list. And yet no one had worked harder to ensure success. He was absolutely saturated with the theory and literature of golf, and could rattle off the roster of open and amateur champions with the fluency of a prize Sunday-school scholar reciting the names of the kings of Judah and Israel. He neglected nothing in the way of precept or practice, and when the club champion got married he had even thought of following his example for its possible effect upon his game. But when he ventured to propose the expedient to Miss Kitty Crake he met with a decided rebuff.

"I shall never," said Miss Crake, "marry a man who is not on the scratch list. When you have won the Hong-Kong Medal, why then we shall see."

Of course, such an answer could be nothing less than the most absolute of refusals. Even in his wildest dreams he had never hoped to come in better than fourth in the monthly handicaps, and that too with an allowance of thirty-six strokes. It is true that there were other young ladies who might have accepted a less heroic standard of excellence than the winning of the Hong-Kong, but Henry Alderson felt that the matrimonial experiment was not worth trying unless Kitty Crake could be induced to take part in it. And so there the matter rested.

When Mr. Alderson stepped to the teeing-ground that afternoon for his first drive he felt unaccountably cool and collected, in spite of the fact that Miss Crake stood in the very forefront of the "gallery." It was one hundred and seventy-seven yards to the first hole, and he usually "hooked " his ball into the "Punch-bowl " hollow at the left, or else feebly topped it along the ground in the one consuming desire to get away from the spectators. But today there should be another tale to tell. For an instant he thought of directing the magic ball to land upon the putting-green dead at the hole, but he reflected that such a phemonenal stroke would undoubtedly be put down as a fluke. It was the part of wisdom to go quietly, and so he picked out a spot some twenty yards short of the green, but in good line, and affording a generous "lie."

As he lifted his club and swung through he was uncomfortably conscious of having transgressed at least eighteen out of the twenty-three cardinal precepts for correct driving, but already the ball was on its way, and, amidst a hearty burst of applause, led, as he could see, by Kitty Crake, it fell precisely as he had determined. A skilful approach laid him dead, and the hole was his in three. A subdued buzz ran around the circle of the "gallery," and everybody bent forward to watch his second drive across the "Punch-bowl." Straight over the yawning hollow flew the ball, and the crowd clapped again; but the play was now too far away to watch, and there were others ready to drive off. Henry Alderson disappeared in the direction of the "meadow" hole, and Miss Crake went to the club-house piazza to make tea. "Poor fellow," she thought, "his foozling will be all the worse when it does come."

It was a very successful tournament, and Henry Alderson won it by the credible score of eighty net. He blushed as the President handed him the silver cross, but the spectators clapped vigorously; for he had always been a good fellow, albeit a bad golfer, and his victory was a popular one.

"Splendid!" said Miss Kitty Crake, and Henry Alderson ascended forthwith into the seventh heaven.

During the month that followed there were some tremendous surprises in store for the record-holders. Three days after the handicap Alderson did the course in eighty-two, thereby breaking the amateur record, and that same afternoon he tied the best professional score. The Green Committee promptly reduced him to the scratch list, and there was some informal talk of sending him to represent the club at the National Amateur meeting. Montague, the holder of the Hong-Kong Medal for two years running, was visibly uneasy. He began to spend more time on the links, and held surreptitious conversations with Alderson's favorite caddie.

But there was a friend as well as an enemy to keep close watch upon Henry Alderson. There was a change in him that only Kitty Crake noticed at first—a change that both annoyed and alarmed her. The becoming modesty with which he had achieved his first successes had entirely disappeared. Almost imperceptibly he had grown self-sufficient and opinionated, and his attitude towards his fellow players was at times little short of offensive. He seemed to take an insolent delight in openly flouting the hoary traditions of the game, and in giving the lie direct to each and every venerable truism incrusted in golfing lore. He invariably used a wrong grip; he played with a full swing for all distances, including the shortest of putts, and he never under any circumstances condescended to keep his eye upon the ball. It was maddening to his fellow-golfers, but his scores were a sufficient answer to all remonstrances. Indeed, it may be said that his steadily decreasing averages

Henry Alderson boasted of his feat, accomplished with a wooden putter. *(&#169 todd olson, courtesy of iStock)*

were beginning to cause the Green Committee considerable uneasiness. For a player to return cards of sixty-four and then fifty-six and then forty-nine seemed to argue unfavorably for the sporting character of the links. Such kind of play was plainly injuring the reputation of the club, and at least the Honorary Secretary was emboldened to hint as much. The very next day Henry Alderson returned a total of eighteen for the full round of holes, and handed it with a mocking smile to the Honorary Secretary himself. This was too much, and Henry Alderson was promptly summoned to appear before the outraged majesty of the Green Committee. But it all ended in smoke. No one could deny that extraordinary scores of a hole in one stroke had been made on several occasions, and in this case it was simply an established phenomenon multiplied by itself eighteen times. "And, gentlemen," concluded Henry Alderson. "I did it all with a wooden putter."

The Green Committee had nothing more to say, but they were plainly dissatisfied, and at once set about putting in some new hazards.

And yet—will it be believed?—Henry Alderson was not a happy man. Egotistical and arrogant as he had become, he yet could not fail to perceive that he had lost immensely in the esteem of his clubmates. Nobody cared to play a match with him; and although at first he had put it down to jealousy, he was gradually forced to admit to himself that the reason lay deeper. Worst of all, Kitty Crake was decidedly cool in her manner towards him. He could not understand it, for his golf was certainly above reproach, and he knew that nothing now could prevent him from winning the Hong-Kong Medal. Once it was pinned upon his breast he would be in a position to demand an explanation and the fulfilment of her promise. But there was still another reason for his wishing that the match was over. Strange as it may appear, the very name of golf had become an abhorrence to him. And yet it was not so strange, after all, when one stops to consider. There is nothing so tiresome as perfection, and this especially applies to golf, as possessing an essentially feminine nature. It is the capriciousness, the inconstancy, of golf that makes it a folly so adorable, and Henry Alderson's game had arrived at a pitch of intolerable perfection. He had long ago discovered that the ball would not be a party to a poor shot. Goaded into fury by the monotonous consistency of his play, he had tried the experiment of ordering the ball into a bunker, or at least a bad lie. But the soulless piece of gutta-percha would have none of his foozling. It simply would not be denied, and after a few trials Henry Alderson resigned himself to his fate, comforting himself with the reflection that, having won the medal (and Kitty Crake), he would give up golf forever.

The day of the contest for the Hong-Kong Medal had come at last, and all golfdom had assembled to see the battle. A round-robin protesting against the admission of Henry Alderson as a competitor had been presented to the Green Committee, but that autocratic body had decided to ignore the protest. "It will be better," said a wise man, "to let him win rather than to give him a handle for a grievance. Let him take the medal, and then we can settle upon some pretext to expel him from the club. Montague has had detectives on the case, and thinks he can prove that Alderson has been playing tennis within the last two months. That will be sufficient in the eyes of all true golfers."

As it happened, Alderson and Montague were paired for the great event, and, of course, they had the gallery with them. Just before they started Alderson mustered up his courage and walked over to where Kitty Crake was standing. She did not raise her eyes as he approached, and he was obliged to speak twice before he could gain her attention.

"I trust that I am to have the benefit of your good wishes," he said, meaningly.

She looked at him in frosty surprise.

"I don't think that they will help you much." And then, with cutting deliberation, "I devoutly wish that the Hong-Kong Medal had never existed."

"Mr. Montague and Mr. Alderson," called out the referee. The two contestants came forward, and Kitty Crake ostentatiously turned her back as the play began.

In all the annals of the Marion County Golf Club a closer and more exciting match had never been played. Montague was certainly putting up the game of his life; and Alderson, while not showing any phenomenal work, was nevertheless returning a faultless score. Not a mistake had been made on either side, and at the end of the seventeenth hole honors were exactly even. But Montague was visibly breaking under the strain.

When Montague stepped forward to drive for the home hole it was plain that he was very nervous. Twice he tried to tee his ball, but his trembling fingers refused their office, and he was obliged to call upon a caddie for assistance. As he came up for the "address " he was deathly pale, and little beads of sweat were standing upon his forehead. The club swung back, and then descended upon the ball, but with a feeble, crooked blow that "sliced" it hopelessly into the bushes. A groan went up. Montague had "cracked," and the match was lost.

Up to this point Henry Alderson had played as though in a dream. At last he understood—those cold, stinging words of Kitty Crake could have but one meaning. *She did not wish him to win!* It was only too plain that she had never loved him, and that she regretted her idle words about the winning of the medal and the promise that they implied. What was he to do?

One thing was certain: he had no chance, in any event, with Kitty Crake. Of course he might go on and win the medal, and then humiliate her by contemptuously refusing to press his claim; but the revenge was an unmanly one, and he could not bring himself to adopt it. Again, he might withdraw, and so give the prize to Montague. He knew that the latter was desperately anxious to retain possession of the trophy. It was the pride, the joy, the treasure, of his otherwise empty life. The Montague infants had all cut their teeth upon the medal's firm and glittering edge. It was the family fetich; the one thing that distinguished them from the common herd of their neighbors, who lived in precisely the same pattern of suburban villa, but whose interest in life never rose above the discussion of village improvements or the election of a vestryman. Henry Alderson hesitated; his heart grew soft within him. And yet to give it up after it had cost him so much!

"Oh yes, a fair enough player, but a trifle short in his driving."

It was Montague who spoke, and Henry Alderson felt instinctively that the remark referred to him. His cheeks burned as he heard the half-veiled insult that only a golfer can understand in its full significance, and he incontinently forgot all about his generous resolution to withdraw. He stepped up to the tee.

"I dare say I can reach the green in two," he said, carelessly.

The hole was some four hundred yards away, and Montague smiled sarcastically. His enemy was about to be delivered into his hands.

"I've done two hundred and forty yards of straight carry," continued Alderson.

"Hym!" coughed Montague.

"And I'd back myself to make it three hundred."

"Why not four?" said Montague.

"Six hundred, if you say so," returned Alderson, hotly.

"Or perhaps out of sight," sneered Montague.

"Off the earth," retorted Alderson.

Montague made no reply, but turned away to hide his satisfaction. Alderson was deliberately going to "press," and every student of the art of golf knows what that implies. But there is nothing more uncertain than a certainty—in golf.

Henry Alderson swung down upon the ball. Shades of St. Rule! but was there ever such a mighty drive? Three hundred yards away, and it was still rising into the blue ether. Another instant and it had passed entirely out of sight, lost in infinite space. The spectators gasped, and Montague turned livid. But stop a bit. Where *was* the ball? The referee looked puzzled, and the caddies stared open-mouthed into the sky. And then in a flash it dawned upon Henry Alderson that his boast had been literally made good. *He had driven his ball off the earth.*

For a moment his heart stood still. With the ball was gone his golfing reputation, and gone forever. Was there anything else for him in life? The answer came in another flash of inspiration. Yes; he was a free man; now he could play golf again—his *own* game. Forgotten was the Hong-Kong Medal;

forgotten for the nonce was Kitty Crake herself. The fit was upon him—the berserker rage of the true duffer. He turned to the referee.

"I acknowledge," he said, "the penalty for lost ball, and play a new one."

He teed a ball, an ordinary gutta-percha, and, swinging down upon it, made the most bungling of "tops." A roar of laughter went up, and Henry Alderson joined in it, the heartiest of all. He caught Kitty Crake's eye, and she was smiling too. Taking a brassey, he advanced for his second shot, and "missed the globe" twice running. But what a delightful sensation it was!— this was something like golf.

Finally, he succeeded in playing inside of Montague, who followed with a splendidly played iron shot out of the bushes. Alderson drove into a bunker, and noted, with an exquisite thrill of pleasure, that his ball had buried itself completely in the sand. It took him three to get out, and the crowd applaud- ed. He "foozled" a shot into a clump of evergreens, and Kitty Crake clapped her hands. Montague made a phenomenal approach, and landed his ball dead at the hole. Alderson "hooked" one ball, "sliced" another, and banged a third into the flag, securing a lucky "rub." He missed two short putts, and then managed to hit Montague's ball, holing it, and leaving his own outside. The laughter of the "gallery" gods cleft the skies, and the referee stepped forward.

"Mr. Montague eighty strokes, Mr. Alderson ninety-six. Mr. Montague wins the tournament, and retains possession of the Hong-Kong Medal."

Curiously enough, it seemed as though the applause that followed the announcement was intended for Alderson rather than for the victor. Men with whom he had not been on speaking terms for months crowded around him to shake his hand. From being the most unpopular man in the club he had suddenly become a hero. It was incomprehensible. Last of all came up Kitty Crake. The crowd had drifted away, and they were alone. Her eyes were wet and shining, and she held out her hand. He took it, trembling inwardly.

"Well," said she at length, "the match is over: have you nothing to say to me!"

"But—but I lost it," faltered Henry Alderson.

"Exactly; and in so doing you just managed to save yourself. You have evidently no idea how simply intolerable a champion at golf may be."

"Oh, Kitty—" he began; but they were already at the club-house.

After they were married he told her the whole story.

"But there is one thing I never understood," he concluded, thoughtfully. "If it really were the enemy of mankind, he certainly acted very stupidly in not getting my signature in the good old orthodox way. What had he to show for his side of the bargain?"

"Oh, that is plain enough," answered Mrs. Alderson. "So long as pride continues to be one of the seven deadly sins—"

"Well?"

"Why, the devil is quite justified feeling cocksure of a medal-winner golf. Poor Mr. Montague!"

CHAPTER 16

PLAYING AUGUSTA—HOW I COMPLETED MY QUEST

JOHN SABINO

It took me ten years to receive the invitation to Augusta, but I finally managed to do it in style. When I created my list of a dozen ways to play I made it a baker's dozen, and it was a good thing. The thirteenth method was to be invited by a former champion, and that is how it happened. Some friends to whom I am forever indebted introduced me to a former winner and we got to know each other. When he learned what I was trying to accomplish he invited me out to play the day before the 2013 Masters. If his name wasn't redacted I wouldn't have revealed it anyway, because it is one of the nicest things anyone has ever done for me and my idea of paying him back doesn't include having him receive letters from legions of eager golfers asking for invitations to play. As I have said, it would not work; you need to be introduced.

For those of you who waded through the whole book in the hope I would tell you who it was exactly, my apologies. You should have been able to tell early on I was a fool, particularly when I gave you my feelings about the Old Course; you should have pitched the book right then and there.

After I was invited to play it took days for me to come back down to earth. Because I am a little anal and, clearly, I have an affinity for lists, I immediately began to keep three: 1) People who were previously my friends who told me they now hated me from jealousy; 2) People who offered to caddie for me, if needed; and 3) People who wanted "Augusta National" and not "Masters" logo items you can only buy in the pro shop in the clubhouse. Sleeping the night before playing was restless, at best (more like hopeless), the sense of anticipation, crushing. Sitting in my hotel room prior to leaving for the round, I was a clinical example of adult ADHD, and displayed all the symptoms in classic form: inattention, hyperactivity, and impulsiveness. I was babbling, moving papers around the room senselessly, and not listening to a word my patient wife said.

On the appointed day the weather was agreeable, about seventy-two degrees, with brilliant sunshine and the gentlest of breezes. I drove over from Atlanta with my generous host, who is one of the true gentlemen of the game. He regaled me with his Augusta stories and how he managed to win the tournament, and all it means to him. As we pulled up to the club's gate off Washington Road, the guard stepped out and recognized him, and we were waved through. What better circumstances are there to play Augusta than as the culmination of a long quest, with the azaleas in bloom, when the course is in tournament condition, and with a Masters champion? Well, none.

I tried to finesse my way onto the course many different ways over the years, and in the back of my mind I knew there was always a possibility I would never play the course. Driving down Magnolia Lane is something I thought might never happen to me, and it would still have been an accomplishment to have played ninety-nine of the top 100 courses in the world, although since I had been to the Masters and walked the course, I would have considered it ninety-nine-and-one-half. I had surgery on my spine a year before playing, had gone into hibernation, and had stopped pressing. It was then that some extraordinarily generous friends introduced me unexpectedly to my future host. The range of emotions I felt being driven under the long canopy of trees was a full spectrum; the most prevalent feelings were joy, fear, excitement, disbelief, exhilaration, and anticipation.

Walking through the door of the plantation-style antebellum clubhouse is as memorable an experience as riding down Magnolia Lane. Having been to the Masters twice, I had already experienced the jaw-dropping awe of the property and its rolling hills. Not that it ever gets old, because it doesn't. Being anywhere on the verdant Augusta grounds is special, no matter how many times you have been there. This time, being able to walk into the clubhouse—an act previously forbidden—was profound, and I had the biggest smile of my life on my face when I entered.

As with everything else in this adult version of Disneyland, the interior of the stately clubhouse is flawless. It is the antithesis of glitz and ostentation; simple, elegant, and the ultimate embodiment of understated Southern charm. There are so many little touches they get right, including a mounted display board in the entry foyer; the board has slots that hold the engraved names of members who are currently on the property, and they slide brass name plates in and out as members arrive and depart. I was trying to act nonchalant and did my best not to gawk at the board, but recognized a couple of names, including their most famous female member, who was present. The clubhouse, with a two-story veranda around the entire building, was built in 1854. It is a veritable museum because it holds the permanent Masters trophy, historic golf clubs donated from past champions, and a sizable oil painting of President Eisenhower. Ascending the winding stairway leads you to the second floor, which contains the dining room where they hold the Champions dinner each year, and the Champions locker room.

The interior of the clubhouse is as perfect as the course. I am sure they don't paint it every week (right?), but the interiors of the buildings looked as if they were freshly painted. The flooring is polished, the carpets are spotless and look freshly laid, and the lucky people working there are charming and gracious. Inside the clubhouse they do not use an electric vacuum cleaner since the noise would disturb the reserved ambiance; instead, they use an old-school manual push-style that makes no noise. I received a tour of the entire grounds including each of the various buildings they use when they run the Masters. My distinguished player gave me a gift to remember the day by, a brand-new wedge made by Bob Vokey with my name engraved on it, and I put it into my golf bag without further thought. We warmed up on the driving range used during the Masters instead of on the members' driving range.

The former champions play from the back tees, as you would expect, but guests play from the member tees, which play 6,365 yards. Because he is such a class act, my host was hitting off the member tees with me on the 1st hole to make me feel more comfortable. Sir Nick Faldo and his son were teeing off behind us, and the three-time champion started to give us heat and suggested in jest to my partner they would be installing ladies' tees for him soon, since he couldn't handle the tournament tees.

I have obviously played many good golf courses and have teed off at some famous pressure-packed locales such as the Old Course at St. Andrews and at Merion with lunch in progress a few feet away. Hitting my first tee shot at Augusta was the most nerve-racking of all, and shortened both my breath and my backswing; my palms were sweaty and my stomach, full of butterflies. The first drive is over a big swale, and although the fairway is wide, the target area is not, since it narrows between the huge bunker on the right and the towering Georgia pines on the left. Looking back, it was one of the narrowest fairway landing areas on the course. Making contact with the ball on the first tee is harder than it sounds; having my tee shot go its normal distance down the fairway was a bonus.

I played well on the first five holes, then the gravity of the situation hit me and I fell apart for the next four or five. When we reached the 6th tee there were two teenagers on the tee box and a couple of older gentlemen sitting in a golf cart. My playing partner said they were people I should meet and he introduced me. One was Bob Goalby, who won the 1968 Masters, and whose name I recognized because he won in the famous incident when Roberto De Vicenzo was disqualified for signing an incorrect score. The other gentleman was Doug Ford, another winner. They were riding along in a golf cart with what I presumed were their grandkids as their guests, and they let us play through. As we walked back to the tee box I asked what year Doug Ford won, and it was 1957, five years before I was born. I pride myself on knowing golf history and know most of the old-timers' names, even obscure names such as Horton Smith and Ralph Guldahl. I had just met a winner I didn't recognize, or if I did, thought was dead; but Doug was there, alive and kicking. And watching. As I set up to the ball, Goalby shouted over, "No pressure, only three former champions watching," and I pulled my tee shot left on the downhill 165-yard par-3.

I have since researched Doug Ford and found out he was born Doug Fortunato, and he is the oldest surviving winner of the tournament. His victory was come-from-behind, beating Sam Snead, and included holing out a shot from a plugged lie in the bunker on the final hole. In a happy coincidence, it turns out I played Augusta almost 100 years to the day my then-twenty-three-year-old grandmother emigrated through Ellis Island from Naples in April 1913, and it was nice to meet a fellow *paisano* at Augusta. America is the land of opportunity, and I am sure she could have never imagined her future grandson being in such an exalted place.

Just as all roads lead to Rome, all golf leads to the back nine at Augusta on a Sunday afternoon, and I was approaching the final holes of my long journey in just such a spot. The next hour was about to be one of the best in my life, and any golfer's dream.

I swung extra hard on the tee at the difficult 9th hole and pulled my drive so far left it ended up in the swale at the bottom of the hill, on the first fairway. My caddie and I walked down to play my shot and as we did he told me to wait up, someone was on the first tee about to hit, so we stood in the pinestraw between the holes and watched a ball sail by us down the first fairway. I had a good view of the 9th green and I lined up and hit the ball back to my hole. Who comes off the first tee as I am doing so, but Tiger Woods. He sees my playing partner and walks over to say hello. They talk for a few minutes and I am introduced, and he tells Tiger that today's round is the final one in my quest to achieve an obsessive golfer's Holy Grail. We exchange pleasantries and he congratulates me.

My body walks up to the 9th green, but my mind doesn't follow; it was still a thousand miles away as I was trying to comprehend meeting a golf icon. We putt out on No. 9 and walk to the 10th tee. We both hit our shots down the massive hill and are off to play the back nine. Except we're not.

The practice putting green is near the 10th tee at Augusta. Two-time winner José María Olazábal, who, at the time, was the current victorious Ryder Cup captain, walks up to the tee and says, "Do you mind if I join you on the back?" My playing partner says, "No problem with me. John, Is it okay if he joins us?" What am I going to say? "No, I'm in a groove, why don't we continue as a twosome." The fairy tale continues.

I hit my drive on No. 10 as good as I could, and my ball was down the hill in the center of the fairway. Meeting Tiger and having José María join us was too much for me to take in and I started to lose it. My caddie was a veteran and helped me calm down; he told me it didn't matter how I played or what score I shot, to relax and enjoy it. Not that he was immune to it; he was shaking his head and said he couldn't believe what was happening, either. I am an average golfer, with a fifteen handicap, and if there is one hope I had going into the round it was to play Amen Corner well. Due to the coaching from the caddie, I regained a sense of calm as I walked onto the 11th tee. Being able to hit the same shots the professionals hit is a dream every golfer

Augusta National, 11th hole. *(John Sabino)*

has. One of the highlights of my life was hitting the middle of the par-4 11th green in regulation (the hole plays 400 yards from the member tees) with a shot that received a simultaneous "great shot" shout-out from two former tournament winners. My birdie attempt was captured by my alert caddie, who knew the gravity of the moment, and took the camera out of my golf bag without being asked. I rolled it to within six inches and was not disappointed with a tap-in par to start Amen Corner.

Standing on the par-3 12th tee I mentally blocked out the water, the ultra-shallow green, the bunkers in the front and in back, the azaleas, the television tower, and everything else. I adjusted for the one-club wind, visualized the shot, saw only the flag, and took a purposeful deep breath. I ended up hitting one of the best shots of my life, eight feet from the hole. This is the reason you stand on the range year after year and hit tens of thousands of practice balls—so when you need to, you can pull off the shot of your life, and it was satisfying. On No. 12 the member tees and the pro tees are in the same place, so I had the exact same shot they hit during the Masters, a 155-yarder over Rae's Creek. Walking over Hogan Bridge is something that cannot be described; it is as good as you think it will be, and a solemn, almost spiritual experience. My putt broke a good cup and a half, and when I heard it land in the bottom of the hole for a birdie, it was hard to absorb. I have had my ups and downs with my golf game over the years, but it was satisfying to birdie what Jack Nicklaus calls "the hardest hole in tournament golf." My host parred the hole and José María hit a high slice into Rae's Creek and ended up with a double-bogey. Not bad, beating two green jacket winners from the same tee box. Walking off the green, José María turned to me and said sarcastically, with a huge smile on his face, "You know John, you should stop showing off, you're making us look bad." If you were to imagine what hole you would want to birdie in the entire world of golf, this would be on the short list. Perhaps the par-3 16th at Cypress, the 17th at TPC Sawgrass, Pebble Beach's 18th, or the Old Course's Road Hole would come to mind too, but No. 12 at Augusta ain't bad.

I was one-under through two holes on Amen Corner, and hit a drive straight down the middle of the 13th fairway. I didn't so much walk over Nelson Bridge as I did float over it. My luck ran out when my ball rolled back off the 13th green and I took a bogey on the hole, but I was still over-joyed, having just lived a golf fantasy. When Herbert Warren Wind coined the phrase "Amen Corner," he described it as your second shot on the 11th, the entire 12th, and your tee shot on the 13th. In the original true sense of Amen Corner, I played it to near perfection.

I am blessed, and for some reason the golf gods were good enough to let me play respectably at Augusta. As is typical, I had my ups and downs. I hit my tee shot on No. 16 into the pond, pulled my ball through the Eisenhower Tree on the 17th, hit my fair share of chip shots fat, and three-putted more than normal because the greens were tournament speed.

A picture you can't take as a spectator at the Masters: the 13th hole from the tee. (*John Sabino*)

My biggest embarrassment of the day was on the par-5 15th hole. I hit a good drive left and laid up my second shot to about 100 yards. It is one of the many shots every golfer imagines hitting when they go to the Masters as a spectator. What club would you hit? Will you lay up or go for it? Will you play it safe or hit to the left side of the green? I laid up, and went for the left pin on my third shot. Sir Nick says, "The course is perfection, and it asks perfection." I hit it less than perfect and it rolled back into the first cut in front of the pond. We walked down to the green over Sarazen Bridge and I took out my brand-new Bob Vokey wedge and took a practice swing. I had to hit the ball straight up in the air to have any chance of holding the green, but it didn't look right when I set up to the ball, given the lie. I put the club back into my bag and took out my lob wedge. As I was taking my practice swing, the club slipped out of my hands and flew end-over-end into the middle of the pond in front of the green. Although everyone in my group thought it was funny, at the time I didn't see the humor in it, and was mortified. My lob wedge is now permanently a part of Augusta, laying at the bottom of those renowned murky waters. The only saving grace out of the incident was that it wasn't the new wedge.

The day was made extraordinary by getting to hear stories from my host and from José María about where and how they hit shots en route to their victories. On several holes, they dropped balls and showed me where they had to make putts from. After my last putt dropped on the final hole, I shook hands with two green jacket winners, and my journey across thirteen countries and twenty-three states, which included thirty-eight courses that have hosted significant tournaments, was done. I saved the best experience for last, and walking off the 18th green of Augusta as the last hole to complete my quest was the only way to finish. To say I was in a state of elation is a gross understatement. At that moment, and borrowing from Lou Gehrig's line, I was the luckiest man on the face of the earth.

To cap off the day-to-end-all-days I played the par-3 course and had a drink in the Champions locker room. It is small and intimate, with only three tables that seat four at each. The veranda outside the room overlooks the circular entry drive and Magnolia Lane. The room was full when I entered, and I was able to trade stories with a dozen former champions, just as you would in the grill room of your local club after a round. I saw my buddy Doug Ford again in the locker room, told him about my birdie and found out he birdied the 12th on Sunday en route to his victory, as well. The players were down-to-earth and we talked about the same types of things you talk about after a round with your friends: how poorly you putted or chipped, which holes you played well, et cetera. It was the crowning achievement of my long and very satisfying journey.

The only way the day could have been any better would have been if Chairman Billy Payne came out of a hidden doorway holding a golden chalice, showed me the secret handshake, and offered me a membership. Aside from my minor fantasy, Hollywood couldn't have scripted it any better.

So how is the course to play for an average player? From tee to green there is no rough, so putting your ball in play is not hard. The fairways are generous, they look and feel like carpets, and every lie is perfect. The greens are perfection, no-holds-barred the best in the world. The most difficult shots tee to green are those you have to hit off of pine needles if you are not in the fairway. The real tests at Augusta are chipping, holding your ball on the greens, and putting. The greens are fast, as you would expect. They are significantly harder on the back nine, in my humble opinion. In particular, I found the 13th, 14th, 16th, 17th, and 18th to be similar to putting on the top of a glass table. The players think the 11th is the hardest hole, but since I parred it, I think it rather easy. Personally, I thought the 7th was the hardest because it is tree-lined and plays to an elevated, well-bunkered green that is more uphill than it looks. My favorite hole on the course was the 13th; it is breathtaking and on a scale most golf holes can never achieve. The back tee is one of the most peaceful places in the world and sits in a little alcove in the back of Amen Corner; standing there, one has not a care in the world.

I have a big imagination. You have to, to envision playing Augusta and completing this quest. My experience at Augusta exceeded anything I could have ever imagined. Any one of my experiences that day is remarkable in its own right. Are my descriptions of Augusta hyperbole? Not in the least, when you experienced what I did as the culmination of a long journey and finish at the best place of all.

CHAPTER 17

IF YOU DON'T MIND
MY TELLING YOU . . .

HOLWORTHY HALL

Mr. Valentine Mott, scowling ferociously, made a fierce gesture toward his wife, five miles distant, and removed the hand which he had fitted over the transmitter as soon as the men in the nearest locker unit had begun to sing "How Dry I Am!" in close and execrable harmony. Mr. Mott leaned in utter impatience against the wall, and glowered mercilessly at his distant wife, and forthwith interrupted her in a voice freighted with glucose and saccharin.

"Well, I'm awfully sorry," he said. "Yes, I *know* I promised to come back for lunch; I know all that. . . . I certainly did intend to come back, but . . . Well, you know how it is; I met this man, and he's a good customer of ours and he wants me to play another round with him. I was just getting ready to change my clothes when he . . . Oh, I *could,* but I don't like to offend a man; these big buyers are so touchy sometimes you wouldn't hardly . . . Well, of *course;* but it's the little personal attentions that count. It's a real opportunity to get in solid with him. . . . Well, I don't see exactly how I can get out of it now; he's waiting for me at the first tee this minute. . . . I hope you don't think I'm *enjoying* it; it's a cold-blooded business proposition; we're not really going out for the *golf;* he just sort of wants to walk around for the exercise and talk business between shots. . . . Well, I *would* bring him home, but he wants the exercise. . . . Oh, absolutely! Why, I'll take you anywhere you say;

I hadn't planned anything for to-morrow. . . . Not to-night, dear; I can't go out anywhere to-night. . . . Yes, to-morrow, and any night next week, too. . . . I certainly *don't!* . . . Well, I didn't even expect to play this afternoon, and to-morrow I'll drive you anywhere you . . . Oh, it might easily mean a thousand dollars to me. . . . Yes, a thousand. . . . Just as soon as we finish. . . . Oh, no, I wouldn't do that! The greens committee doesn't like to have women on the course on Saturdays. I'll start home the minute we finish. . . . All right; I'm just as sorry as you are. Goodbye!"

Mr. Mott hung up the receiver, exhaled in an abandon of relief, and smartly accosted a cadaverous friend, who happened to be passing through the locker room.

"Oh, Smithson! Made up yet for the afternoon?" Smithson paused, and shook his head disconsolately.

"I'm sorry, but I've got to go home, Val. Where's the crowd you had this morning?"

"They had to go home, too," said Mr. Mott, implying unutterable weakness on the part of the henpecked miscreants. "*I'm* going to play eighteen more."

"How in thunder do you do it?" asked the cadaverous one in frank envy and injured righteousness. "If I ever managed to get in thirty-six holes just *once—*"

Mr. Mott waved the hand which had recently done duty as a silencer.

"Easiest thing in the world. Mrs. Mott wouldn't any more think of spoiling my Saturdays than—well, she just wouldn't think of it. She knows I'm working like a dog all the week; a man's got to have *some* recreation."

"That's so; but I can't ever seem to get it over. Well, how were you shooting?"

"Pretty fair—for me." Mr. Mott nodded, moved off in the direction of the grill, and halted on the outskirts of a loquacious group which was actively engaged in filing demurrers and replications. "Everybody made up?" he inquired genially. With discouraging unanimity they answered in the affirmative; and in the same breath they asked him how he was traveling.

"Not bad—that is, for me," said Mr. Mott. He hailed a lone wayfarer who was hurrying along the aisle. "Anybody looking for an extra man?"

"Sorry! Say, Val, there's a special competition on for the afternoon; heard about it?"

"No," said Mr. Mott, alert. "What is it?"

"Straight medal-play, handicap. Special prize put up by one of the new-comers. Wasn't on the regular program."

"Is that so? I'll have to see about it. Well, how're you hitting 'em?"

"Vile!" The lone man took up his march in the direction of the attendant's room, and Mr. Mott shook his head in profound sympathy, and went on to the bulletin-board, where he delayed for a moment to inspect the current handicap-list. As he stood there, sniffing contemptuously at his own modest rating, a trio of late arrivals burst through the side door, and bore down upon him, laughing and talking and forecasting the future with that incorrigible golfing optimism which is Phoenix-born everyday out of the black ashes of yesterday's sodden facts. Mr. Mott knew all three, and he hailed them cheerfully.

"Hello! Looking for a fourth man?"

"No; somebody's waiting for us. No competition this afternoon, is there?"

"Of course there is! Special prize for straight medal-play," said Mr. Mott. "Don't you fellows ever read the announcements?"

"Is that so? That's fine! Thought there wasn't anything doing! Well, how were you going this morning?"

"Oh, pretty fair—for me, of course."

The trio hurried away, and Mr. Mott, lingering only to make sure that the tabular results of the competition for the treasurer's cup still remained on the board,—he hadn't been put out until the semifinals, and liked to see his name in the bracket,—strolled into the grill, and cast about him for companionship.

The low-studded room, as Mr. Mott entered, echoed the mad confusion of a political convention crossed with a dairy restaurant. Crockery clattered against wooden surfaces, plated silver clattered against crockery, tumblers clinked to tumblers, and hobnails grated on the red-tiled floor. Men in knickerbockers and men in flannels huddled close to the round tables and bawled statistics at one another; men in street clothes dragged rattling caddy-bags through from the office; men flushed and perspiring stamped in from the eighteenth green, and clamored loudly at the bar. Disheveled waiters dodged aimlessly about in answer to the insistence of a dozen members simultaneously. Half a hundred voices swelled in extenuation, alibi, defense; half a hundred voices rang clear in joyous prophecy. Drifting clouds of light-gray smoke clung like a canopy to the ceiling. The atmosphere was surcharged with excitement, and Mr. Mott's nostrils dilated as he scented it. The air quivered to the ungodly tumult, and Mr. Mott's ear-drums vibrated as he heard it.

"Waiter! Hang that waiter! Here, you! I—"

"I had a putt for a forty-seven coming in; without that nine on the tenth I'd have had a putt for a forty-one—"

"Come on; be a sport; make it a ball Nassau—"

"Why should *I* give you a stroke? Here's *my* suggestion—"

"All right! All right! Count it up yourself! 5, 7, 4, 9, 6, 6, 8—"

"Five aces in one! *I'*ll stand!"

"Hey, Jim! I had a par five—"

"Waiter! Waiter! I didn't order soup!"

"That's ground under repair. It says so on the card—"

"Oh, I couldn't hit a balloon. Worst I *ever* did!"

"Well, if you start us one up on each nine and—"

"Confound it! *I* didn't make the rules! It costs you two strokes!"

"Telephone! Telephone for Mr. Smithson! Mrs. Smithson calling—"

"Well, my handicap's too low. He's been under ninety twice this year, and the best I ever made in my life was a ninety-four, and still I've got to give him three strokes—"

"*Waiter!* Hurry along that club sandwich, will you?"

"If you'd just keep that left shoulder down, Bill, and remember to follow through—"

"I'll *bet* you I break 110—"

"Oh, if I could putt, I'd be all right. I just can't putt."

"Here, give *me* that check! Oh, come now; that's not right—"

"Then I went all to pieces—"

"Well, if I'd been playing my game—"

"Honest, I'd like to play you even, but I haven't touched a club since June—"

"Oh, I was *awful!*—How about you?"

"Waiter!"

Mr. Mott smiled happily, and button-holed the chairman of the handicap committee.

"Made up yet?" he inquired.

The chairman was prone to brevity.

"Yes. How'd you come out this morning?"

"Rotten!" said Mr. Mott, promptly. "Tore up my card; I was fierce. Know anybody that's looking for a match?"

"Yes, there's a new member out by the caddy-house. Don't know who he is, but he's alone. I thought somebody ought to give him a welcome. *You* do it, Val."

"Good idea—I will." Mr. Mott edged his way to the outer door, bellowed over his shoulder to one who had bellowed a question at him—the answer was "Pretty fair—for me!"—and emerged to the gravel walk. At this hour the vicinity of the first tee was deserted, but before the professional's tiny house Mr. Mott saw a lanky stranger dallying in an attitude of longing; Mr. Mott drew near and grinned. The stranger looked up, and presently grinned in return.

"Waiting for somebody?" asked Mr. Mott.

"No," said the stranger. "Just taking my chances; I'm a new member."

"Indeed! My name's Mott."

"Chapman's mine."

They shook hands. Mr. Mott glowed with the consciousness of duty well done.

"I'm alone, too. Suppose we try it?"

"I'd be glad to. Your name up for the handicap?"

"Not yet."

"I'll put it up," volunteered Mr. Mott. In the top space on the ruled sheet tacked to the scoreboard he scrawled his own patronymic, and added his stroke allowance. "What's yours?"

"They haven't given me one. I've been in the club only a week."

"*Well,*" said Mr. Mott, uncertainly, "then you can't very well compete—"

"Oh, I'm not going to. I'm not strong for tournaments, anyway. If you don't mind, I'll just attest your round; I'm not in condition anyway."

"All right." Mr. Mott dusted his hands, and stepped over to the caddy-master. "A couple of boys ready? Who do I draw? This one? My bag there? Now, son, your job is to *watch the ball.* You remember that, will you? Let's have the driver." He strode within the fatal inclosure, and swung the club experimentally at a trespassing cigarette stub. The stub leaped forward a yard, accurately on the line. "What do you play around in?"

"Oh, I'm erratic," said Chapman, watching intently. "You take the honor, please."

"Well, if you say so." He chuckled. "Might as well take it when I can get it. I may never have another chance." He teed an almost new ball, and took his stance; waggled, hesitated, stooped, glanced at his caddy, and glared at him. "Another ball," he said shortly. "Red-line Silver King out of the pocket." The caddy, overwhelmed with guilt, furnished it. It was of the same brand, the same marking, the same weight, and showed the same degree of wear and tear as the original choice; but Mr. Mott, for reasons comprehended only by golfers, regarded it with far greater satisfaction. It was the ball with which he had made the last hole in a par five on the morning round. It was, so to speak, already broken in, trained, biddable. Mr. Mott teed it, and after swinging once or twice in exaggeratedly correct form, lunged downward savagely.

"Good ball!" approved Chapman.

"Too high," said Mr. Mott, with meretricious disgust. It was the longest drive he had made from the first tee in six weeks.

The stranger hit a prodigious hook out of bounds. On his second attempt the hook was less pronounced; he was in the rough. The two players set out fraternally on their journey.

"Been playing much lately?" inquired Mr. Mott.

"Not a great deal. Only once or twice since April."

"You've got a fine follow-through, though."

"Unfortunately, there's more to the game than that," deprecated Chapman. He selected a spoon, and was hole-high to the left of the green.

"Beautiful! Just a trifle off," commented Mr. Mott. With the sole of his club he patted down a worm-cast; with his heel he deleted a tuft of grass from the complications of his lie. He made his effort, and afterwards he held himself rooted to the spot until he had verified, by three swings at vacancy, his unexpressed opinion that, given another opportunity, he would have split the flag, instead of dubbing fifty feet downhill. "I can't keep my head down," he lamented. "Oh, well—" He turned suddenly to his caddy, and sent a bolt of lightning at him. "*Watch* this one!" he ordered. And the caddy obediently watched it hobble a hundred yards, and disappear among the leaves of a dry trench.

As Mr. Mott, looking aggrievedly at a pair which had come up behind him and were yelling "Fore!" at the top of their lungs, stood on the first green and noted his score, he was impelled to quote history.

"I had a six here this morning," he sighed. "It's a tricky green, isn't it?"

"Very," agreed his partner. "You keep the honor all the way, will you? You're in the tournament, and I'm not."

"Just as you say. On this one you want to aim pretty well to the left of the mound." Mr. Mott drove thirty yards to the right of it. "Doggone it!" he exclaimed, with his hands on his hips, "that club's no earthly good; I can't hit the broad side of a barn with it! It isn't balanced, or something. Further to the left, Mr. Chapman." Here Chapman sent forth a towering drive which at least was out of trouble. "*That's* safe! You're lucky."

"Oh, I'm not kicking," said Chapman placidly. "But I'm afraid you're in the pit."

"I see," said Mr. Mott, getting into his stride, "that Bobby Jones hasn't been doing as well this season as he did last. Well, that's the way it ought to work out. He's too young to have all that success; it might have spoiled him. Besides, the national's no place for a boy like that. I was hoping he wouldn't go too far at Merion a year ago."

"He made a seventy-four," said Chapman, shrugging his shoulders, "and a seventy-six and a seventy-seven—"

"Oh, that's not so very remarkable. You take these caddies; they watch good players, and get hold of a good swing, and they're not bothered with nerves—"

"Pardon me, but I think you're back there about ten yards, Mr. Mott."

"So I am! Much obliged! Fore!"

Within a quarter of a mile there was no one who might conceivably have been endangered by Mr. Mott's recovery from the sand-pits, but his warning cry was both mechanical and peremptory. He eyed the flag, three hundred yards in advance, and with his eye still on it he played the mashie-niblick in the stroke which made Edward Ray internationally famous. It made Mr. Mott apoplectic. Thenceforward he progressed by slow and circuitous stages to the sloping green, and upon his arrival he was too deeply perturbed to sympathize with Chapman, whose iron shot had found a trap, and whose approach was beyond the hole. To be sure, the sinking of a long putt did much to salve the irritation in Mr. Mott's bosom, and although Chapman also holed a twenty-footer, Mr. Mott secretly felt, and generously withheld the statement, that Chapman had been excessively fortunate in the roll of the green. And he was too much absorbed in his own cosmos to inquire Chapman's score.

The third hole was short; that is, it was short for scratch-players. Mr. Mott had seen Tommy Kerrigan, the club professional, once play it with a heavy mashie; he had seen Sumner Hollander, who, although rated at nine, was Mr. Mott's ideal performer, overplay it with a mid-iron. Therefore Mr. Mott, who, if he could have reached the pin with a full brassey once out of three trials, would have owed sacrifices to the gods and blessings to a beam wind, chose a mid-iron.

"I'm not generally as bad as this," he explained when the ball had found cover in a growth of underbrush. "I'm not getting my wrists into it, that's all. I don't know what's the matter with me today. I don't seem to have any snap. It's costing me a stroke a hole, too."

"Easily," said Chapman. He, too, was off the line, but he was near enough to the green to use a putter while Mr. Mott was still flailing at the underbrush, and he was down in four to Mr. Mott's six.

"Now for a long one," complained Mr. Mott, climbing the eminence to the fourth tee. "Well, I suppose I'll have to take that driver of Kerrigan's again. If I had any sense I'd drive with an iron. Well, never mind. I believe in playing the right club. Watch it, boy!" He hit a screaming liner down the alley for more than two hundred precious yards, and posed diligently and without motion, until the ball had not only come to rest, but had also lain quiescent for several seconds. He regarded the club-head in general perplexity. He tested the spring of the shaft. He breathed deeply, and made way for Chapman; and after Chapman, owing to a half-top, had failed by a full rod to equal that drive of Mr. Mott's, he relentlessly fought down the smile which struggled for its outlet. Indeed, he was rather astonishingly severe and unemotional for a man who had just accomplished a praiseworthy feat, and got back on his game. He endeavored by conversation to disguise his glory.

"You've just joined the club, Mr. Chapman?"

"Only a week ago, Mr. Mott."

"Pretty nice course, don't you think? It's very hard. It's harder by three strokes than any other course in the metropolitan district, and the fairway's a bit ragged, and the greens are pretty nearly hopeless; but you wait five years! I tell you, a man's got to keep out of the rough on this course or he's dished. I like a stiff course; it's the only kind to have. Where did you play formerly?"

"Over in Boston—Woodland."

"Oh! Do you know Francis Ouimet?"

"I should say I do! Do *you?*"

"Well, not personally," said Mr. Mott, with some haste. "But of course . . . if he had more time to play, he'd be a wizard, wouldn't he? Fore!"

"You're in the pit!" shrilled Mr. Mott's caddy.

"Well, don't tell me about it *now!*" roared Mr. Mott, turning livid. He glanced at Chapman. "Excuse me, I thought you'd played. Well, of all the—" He saw Chapman's stinging brassey, which had threatened to sail into a grove of pines to westward, suddenly veer to the east, and drop lazily abaft the green.

"Pretty lucky," said Chapman. "I played for a slice, but—"

"*Lucky!* I wish I had *half* your luck! I'd be down to a three handicap, by gosh! See my ball anywhere, caddy? You said it was in the pit."

The boy indicated it.

"It bounced over, sir."

"Humph!" said Mr. Mott, accepting the gift of the fates without evident thankfulness. "Well, why don't you *watch* it, boy? Tell me it's in the pit, and then . . . stand still, will you? Stop rattling those clubs!" He hit a high iron and lost it in the sun. "Say, I didn't see that one at all."

"Neither did I," said Chapman. "But it sounded like a clean hit."

Mr. Mott shifted the responsibility to his faithful retainer, who was non-chalantly chewing gum.

"Did you mark it, caddy?"

"No, sir; couldn't see it drop. Sun's in my eyes." Mr. Mott snorted, and tossed his cleek to the ground.

"Good Lord!" he snapped. "What d'you think you're paid for? D'you think I hire you to *lose* balls? Anybody can carry the clubs; your job is to *watch* the *ball!* Why didn't you mark it? That'll make three I've lost today, and you—"

"It's on," stated the caddy, chewing rapidly.

"*On!* Where?"

"On the green. Over by the sprinkler."

Mr. Mott coughed delicately, and looked at Chapman under his lashes. Chapman wasn't on; Chapman wasn't on by a good ten yards, but Mr. Mott was on in three, and the hole was a par five.

"I've got a chance for a birdie," he whispered to himself, "a chance for a four. It's four hundred and eighty yards, and I've got a chance for a four. For a birdie. . . . *Good shot!*" Chapman had clipped up neatly.

Mr. Mott took his putter, and made an awkward jab at the ball. It fled at a disconcerting angle. Mr. Mott flushed, pursued the gutty, and jabbed again. Then he lifted himself erect, and poured out into the world the offscourings of his innermost soul. He reviled himself, the Silver King golf-ball, the Vaile putter, the greenskeeper, the turf, the contour of the land, the Scotch who had invented the game, and the promoters who had organized the club. As an afterthought, he hurled the putter into a convenient hazard, and, seizing the first weapon which came to hand—a niblick—struck so fair and true that the ball went down for a six, one over par.

"Too bad!" said Chapman. "I missed an easy one, myself."

"I had a chance for a four," declared Mr. Mott, loudly. "Of all the rotten putting I ever saw in my *life* that was the worst! On the green in three, and three putts! These greens are rotten! Worst in the world; and believe me, I've seen some bad ones! Where's my driver? Hurry up, there!"

While his mood was of grim resolution, and he concentrated rigidly upon the act, he drove off in excellent form and with highly creditable results.

"There!" he ejaculated. "*Now* I'm getting back on my game. That old war-club certainly does poke 'em out when I hit 'em right. But three putts, and only one over par at that! If our greens were as good as they've got at Wykagyl or Sleepy Hollow—"

He observed that his companion had again hooked, and by virtue of his own superiority of direction he was vastly exhilarated. The second shots, too, filled him with passionate joy, for he was safely over the brook, while Chapman had pulled into tall grass. Mr. Mott sidled toward his partner, and made diplomatic overtures of assistance.

"If you don't mind my telling you," he said, "you stand too far back of the ball. You can't help hooking when you do that. You push the face of the club right across the ball. It's like a masse shot in billiards. You're getting good distance, but you hook all the time. Just straighten 'em out and you'll be 'way out every time. Stand farther ahead, and you'll be all right."

"I certainly am hooking 'em," acknowledged the lanky man.

"Well, if you don't mind my telling you—"

Mr. Mott's shots put him safely over the brook. *(Curt Pickens, courtesy of iStock)*

"Not a bit!"

"More like this," said Mr. Mott, illustrating. "Go back slower, and let go with your right hand at the top of the swing. Then take hold hard with your left when you start to come down. It's the left hand that does the business. And follow through more. Now, you take that last shot of mine; I hit three inches behind the ball, and the follow through saved it. All of it was bad but the follow through; but what happened? It went as straight as a die. Say, are those people going to stay on that green all *night?* Fore!"

"Oh, they haven't holed out yet."

"Yes, they have; they're counting their scores. Some people don't realize there's such a thing as etiquette in this game. *Fore!*"

He topped into the brook.

"Fore!" said Mr. Mott, waving his niblick.

He hammered the ball into a bank of yielding clay.

"Fore!" rasped Mr. Mott, setting his teeth.

He essayed a pitching stroke, a lofting stroke, an extricating stroke, and two shoveling strokes, and the last of these brought him to solid earth.

"Fore!" shouted Mr. Mott, wild-eyed. He ran an approach to the edge of the green and panted violently. "Four—and I'm on in five," said Mr. Mott, utterly innocent. "Where'd *you* go?"

"Just off—over by the water-pipe."

Mr. Mott exhaled luxuriously, and fanned himself with his hat.

"That isn't bad. One of you boys take the flag. Good work!" Secretly he held that Chapman's run-up was a fearful fluke.

"Sink it now," urged Chapman, encouragingly.

Mr. Mott tried his best to sink it, and missed by a bare inch.

"Throw that back here!" he ordered.

The second endeavor was flawless. Legally, Mr. Mott had taken two putts; morally, he had taken one—the last one. It was this consciousness of innate ability, this realization that if he had aimed a hair's-breadth farther to the left he would have sunk the first attempt that cheered and inspired him. He could have done it if he had really cared about it. And Chapman missed a two-footer!

"If you don't mind my telling you," said Mr. Mott, with admirable restraint, "you can putt a whole lot better if you turn the face of your putter over toward the hole. It puts a drag on the ball. It makes it run close to the ground. I had a six; no, seven. That first one should have gone down. Seven."

"Twelve," said his caddy, apprehensive, but judicial.

Mr. Mott turned upon him vehemently.

"*Twelve!* What in thunder are you talking about? Five on the green—"

"No, sir, ten—"

"Listen! Three in the brook,—" Mr. Mott's mouth opened slowly, and his jaw fell,—"three in the brook," he repeated in horror, "and—"

"And nine out, sir. You yelled 'Fore!' and counted the next stroke five—"

"Give me the mid-iron," said Mr. Mott, abruptly. "Get down there and mark this shot!" He wheeled to gaze at the scene of his recent dredging operations. "Three in the brook, four, five, six, seven—*Hey! Stop swinging those clubs!* Well, I *said* it was seven! Three in the brook—"

"Your honor, Mr. Mott."

"Thank you." He teed for the short sixth across a threatening ravine. "*Caddy,* wake up there!" He turned to his partner with a gesture of Christian resignation. "Don't you wish," he asked, "that just once in a while you'd find a caddy that showed some *interest* in the game?"

The sixth hole was a trifling matter of a hundred and fifty yards; but to render it attractive to experts, there were mental, physical, and psychological hazards cunningly placed by nature, aided and abetted by Donald Ross. As Mr. Mott wavered on the tee, he saw a deep gully, weed-infested and spotted with frowning rocks; he saw pits limiting and guarding the green; he saw trees and excavations and a stone wall. Upon its misshapen mound of sand he saw the Silver King waiting resignedly for its certain punishment. He saw his mid-iron, broad bladed and heavy, a club capable of propelling thirty pennyweight of rubber and silk an eighth of a mile and more if properly coerced. Yet Mr. Mott discounted the inherent qualities of that iron, just as he discounted the elasticity of the golf-ball and the power of his wrists and forearms. He recalled that on the last few occasions of his attack upon this hole he had shafted his ball over the stone wall, and he wondered dumbly how he might prevent a repetition of the error. Instinct warned him to go for the hole, and play with assurance; but for several minutes he hadn't been on good terms with his instinct. He struggled to revive the warnings of those who have written text books, to remember what Taylor or Braid or Travers has prescribed as antidotes for shafting tee-shots. "Stop talking!" he growled at the caddies. "How d'you think I can drive when you're talking!" Out of the obscurity of printed words a phrase flashed to his brain and he was aware that as Haultain says, he was about to pivot on the head of the left thigh-bone, working in the cotyloidal cavity of the *os innominatum.* He placed the mid-iron in position, and told himself that upon his life he wasn't to move his right gastrocnemius or sartorius except torsionally. He rehearsed, in one mad instant, platitudes affecting the right elbow, the eyes, the left knee, the interlocking grip, and the distribution of weight. He lifted the club stiffly, and brought it down again. Too cramped! He settled himself more comfortably, and peered at the stone wall. The green, half bathed in golden sunshine, half purplish in dense shadow, seemed to reach out yearning arms to draw the Silver King to its broad bosom. A hundred and fifty yards, par three. Mr. Mott caught his breath in a quick intake, and drove sickeningly into the stone wall.

"Oh, tough!" said Chapman.

But the features of Mr. Mott expressed no rage. On the contrary, he was smiling placidly, as a parent smiles at a wayward child. The crisis had come and gone; the most difficult obstacle of the entire round was now a matter of indifference to him; he had known positively that he was destined somehow to entangle himself with that stone wall, and now he had done it. Even so, he didn't begrudge his partner that arching shot which spanned the ravine, and lacked not more than a yard or two of carrying the green; on the contrary, he was glad that Chapman had done so well.

"I *always* dub this hole," he said cheerfully. "I got a two on it last July, but ordinarily I'm satisfied if I get a four. You're well up there; still a tiny bit of a hook, though. But you're doing a lot better since I told you."

"I'm working hard enough to straighten 'em out," deprecated Chapman.

"Well, if you take a nice, easy swing, and don't pull your body round, you'll get good results. I hope you don't mind my telling you."

"Far from it," said Chapman, humbly.

Mr. Mott's caddy pointed to the ball, which was virtually unplayable among the stones. Mr. Mott, now that he had passed the climax of his round, was suddenly dogged and determined. It was all well enough to flub the drive, but this approach of his was serious business. He broke off a reed or two which interfered with his stance; he commandeered both caddies to assist him in the removal of sundry large rocks; he bent the grasses so that he had a fighting chance to smash through with his deep-faced mashie. Down on the green Chapman was watching earnestly. On the sixth tee a fast-moving foursome was emitting comments which blew across the ravine, and caused the muscles of Mr. Mott's jaw to tighten significantly. Duffer, was he! He'd show 'em whether he was a duffer or not! He focused on the flag, and swung the mashie in a wide ellipse.

Mr. Mott, by virtue of that mysterious and extraordinary sense with which some men are sometimes gifted, had known with utter privity of knowledge that he was sure to recover from the rough. There was no doubt about it; it was his destiny. What he hadn't known, or remotely suspected, was that he would cover sixty good yards with that clean swipe, and lose his ball in the wilderness of the adjacent jungle. And even in that moment when he most commiserated with himself for the gross faultiness of the club and the grave defects of the ball, he wasn't nearly so much tortured by the necessity of playing three, still from trouble, as he was by the necessity of allowing that cynical foursome to go through. His gorge rose at the mere conception of being passed; in match-play he would have conceded the hole instanter rather than suffer the ignominy of signaling a foursome to take precedence; but in medal-play he must finish every hole and hole every putt; so that he fretted impatiently for five long minutes, spoke to his caddy in curt mono-syllables, and majestically expelled from the course, as a thief and a pirate, a soiled and tattered renegade who leaned over the wall and offered to sell him two second-hand floaters for a quarter. In days gone by Mr. Mott had bought perhaps two dozen balls from that self-same urchin, that boy who wearily spent the long summer evenings in beating thicket and brush for abandoned gutties; but today he looked askance upon the scoundrel, and saw him plainly for what he was, a trafficker in illicit wares, a golf-hound outlawed and thrice condemned. Besides, last Saturday Mr. Mott had purchased four old balls from him only to discover later that two of them were balls which Mr. Mott himself had lost a fortnight ago. They had his initials on them.

The foursome, completing their routine with incredible speed and skill, disappeared in the middle distance. Mr. Mott played three, and Mr. Mott played four, and if he hadn't kept majestic control over his temper, he would have dumped his clubs in the nearest pit, brained his caddy with a patent putter, and started incoherently for Bloomingdale. As it was, he merely con-firmed the theory that the terminology of masculine hysteria is limited to four suffixes, and played five without caring whether he found the hole or Long Island Sound. As a matter of fact, he found the hole.

"Bully!" said Chapman. "I made mine, too; thought we'd better save time. I putted while you were hunting."

Mr. Mott, red and perspiring, shook his head sadly.

"I ought to have had a four," he maintained. "I wasted a shot. That's eight strokes I've absolutely thrown away this round. I ought to have had a four easy. If you don't mind my telling you, you'd better play straight for the big tree. Then your hook'll make it come around into the fair." Whereupon Mr. Mott hit a very high, very short hook, and as he postured in the guise of Ajax—save that Ajax presumably had no such costume and no such implement to intensify the dramatic value of his gestures—he fervently apostrophized the wind, which had taken a perfectly straight ball and blown it into a trap. He wasn't influenced in his decision by the sight of a marker-flag drooping lazily on its staff, nor by the circumstance that Chapman's drive, which attained almost equal height, came to earth without a single degree of deviation from the line of shortest distance.

"The wind took it right around!" flamed Mr. Mott, snatching his niblick. "Fore!"

It was a good out, and Mr. Mott played a goodly third. His fourth, however, was abortive, although the divot flew gracefully. Mr. Mott withheld his analysis until Chapman had curved an approach within striking distance of the green, and then his finer sensibilities prompted him to disregard himself and to tutor Chapman.

"That was a nice ball," he began sincerely, "but you're still hooking. Why don't you try addressing it with the heel of the club? That makes you come around in after it. You try that, and see what it does. And I've noticed you go back too fast. You can't do that and keep your balance unless you're a good player. Slow back, and crook your left knee more. In at the ball, I mean. Like this!" His delsarte was masterly; and although he foundered the shot, the ball rolled and rolled until it trickled on to the green and stopped dead. "Well,

that's the idea, but I didn't get it up enough," said Mr. Mott with decent reserve. Subsequently they each used the putter twice.

The eighth was a respite, and they halved it in four. On the ninth tee,
to the frank annoyance of another foursome which had overtaken them, Mr.
Mott refused to drive until the quartet ahead had left the green, two hundred
and twenty-two yards away, uphill.

"A good wallop'll carry that far sometimes," he explained with dignity.
"I've done it myself. Almost did it this morning. They're off now, anyway."
Before proceeding to the shot, he condescended to lighten the situation with
a ray of humor. "I'd hate to kill anybody," he said, and after an enormous
swing topped not more than a mallet's length into the tall grass.

From the restive foursome a gruff voice struck harshly upon Mr. Mott's
sensitive ears:

"Well, that was a damn' humane impulse all right!"

With a medal score of sixty-three for the first nine, Mr. Mott bade fare-
well to all thought of a silver trophy for his library, and devoted himself to a
keen study of ballistics as exemplified by his partner's chronic hook. For two
holes he fairly exuded advice and encouragement, but at the twelfth tee he
was staggered to discover that he had counseled an ingrate. Without question, Chapman was improving steadily; the hook was appreciably less, and
Mr. Mott had merely said, with the kindest of motives, that Chapman *was*
improving, and that if he'd only remember to stare while he counted three at
the spot where the ball had rested before he hit it, he'd do even better. And
Chapman, smiling faintly, replied in a gentle tone which contained rebuke:

"Perhaps if you'll play your own game, Mr. Mott, and let me play mine,
we'll get along well enough as it is."

Mr. Mott wouldn't have been human if he hadn't taken seven on the
next hole, and he wouldn't have been human if he hadn't experienced a thrill
of primitive triumph when Chapman not only hooked his drive, but also his
full mid-iron. Granted that his approach was moderately efficient, Chapman
deserved nothing better than a seven, or possibly a six, with divine aid; but
when he putted wretchedly off direction, and the ball, obviously deflected by

the agency of a slope which Mr. Mott hadn't seen and couldn't discern, curled sharply in toward the cup, and tottered to the lip of it, and dropped, Mr. Mott compressed his lips and said nothing. He realized that comment was superfluous; when a man had that sort of luck, which simply compensated for two earlier mistakes, there was nothing for a righteously indignant opponent to say. Chapman had even forfeited his earlier right to be joked about it.

But when Chapman achieved a perfect drive on the thirteenth Mr. Mott burst with information.

"That's the queerest thing I ever saw in my life!"

"What is?"

"Why, that ball was straight as a die! And you stood for another hook!"

"No!" said Chapman.

"But—why, certainly you did. I'd have told you, but you'd begun your swing, and I was afraid of spoiling your shot. It's the funniest thing I ever saw! Where am I, caddy?"

"In the pit," said the stolid caddy.

By the time he got out, he perceived that his companion had finished, and was sitting on the bench in the shade. Highly offended at the discourtesy, Mr. Mott whistled as a demonstration of independence, and utilized an unconscionable length of time in a study of topography. To do him justice, he wasn't seeking to retaliate; he was resolved that by his own excellence in the short game he would display his lack of nerves and his imperturbability in a trying moment. The man whose partner has played out rather than to wait politely while sandpits are under exploration is subject to an adjustment of poise; and although Mr. Mott had the satisfaction of leaving no loophole for criticism, and of holing prettily, he was nevertheless too fundamentally introspective to drive well on the dog-leg fourteenth.

Furthermore, although the region immediately surrounding his ball wasn't placarded as ground under repair when Mr. Mott began his onslaught upon the turf, it was indubitably in need of repair when Mr. Mott got through with it. He quarried out a blanket of gravelly soil at each of four desperate offensives, and when he toiled wearily up the hillside to the rolling green he took two putts for a nine, and was aware that Chapman, whether befriended or betrayed by fortune, hook or no hook, had beaten him by a margin of many strokes.

But the sun was setting, the end was near, and Chapman was a new member. Mr. Mott relaxed somewhat, tore his tournament score-card to bits, and scattered them on the grass.

"No use keeping *that* any more," he said. "I can't putt on these plowed fields they call greens. They're a disgrace to the club, that's what they are. Now, this is what I call a beautiful hole. Four hundred and sixty—over beyond the farthest line of trees. Par five; it ought to be par six."

"Why?"

Mr. Mott was mildly astonished.

"Because it's a hard hole."

"But par's arbitrary, Mr. Mott."

"Yes, but the greens committee—"

"The greens committee hasn't anything to do with it. Any hole up to two hundred and fifty is par three, from that to four fifty is par four, from four fifty-one to six hundred is par five. So this is a par five—and it's only ten yards too long to be a par four."

Mr. Mott blinked at the sun.

"What makes you think that?"

"I don't think it; I *know* it. The U. S. G. A. changed the figures in April, but the ruling didn't affect this particular distance at that."

"Well, I may be wrong, but my impression is that the greens committee fixes the par for the different holes. Anyway, here goes!"

"Nice ball!" said Chapman.

Mr. Mott smiled conciliatingly.

"Tommy Kerrigan made that driver for me," he said. "It's a pippin. As soon as I swing I can *feel* I'm going to hit it clean. I *beg* your pardon! Did I take your mind off your shot?"

"Not at all. I'm out there about where you are."

"It was a screamer," said Mr. Mott, unaware of the inference to be drawn from the compliment. "As good a drive as I've seen in a month."

To his immense gratification, he was hole-high on his second shot, and home on his third. He compelled himself to plan for two putts, to insure himself a par five instead of risking all on a bold steal which might prove, by metamorphosis, to be a gift to the devil. In consequence he very nearly holed out, and he was far too enraptured to care what Chapman got. Chapman had manhandled his chip shot, and Mr. Mott hadn't noticed the others. Let Chapman account for himself. Par five! Who cared what Chapman got?

According to the custom duly laid down in such cases, Mr. Mott took many practice swings on the sixteenth tee. Temporarily, he had struck his head upon the stars, and with the pride of a champion he swung with a champion's ease and freedom. Par five! Mr. Mott, with the image of the Vardon statue hovering before his eyes, clipped bits of turf from the scarred tee and ogled the green. Kerrigan had often overdriven it; once when the ground was baked out; it wasn't much more than two hundred and forty yards. And the rough directly before the tee, the trap to the left, and the rough to the right,

Mr. Mott easily achieved the putt on the sixteenth hole. *(anopdesignstock, courtesy of iStock)*

what were they? Who but novices were to be alarmed by puny obstacles such as these? Surely not the man who has made the long fifteenth in a par five!

"Fore!" he said mechanically.

Mr. Mott drove magnificently, and started hastily over the foot-bridge, then halted at the pleasant laughter of his companion; and shamefacedly stood aside. He never looked to see where Chapman drove; his consciousness was riveted upon a small white object far up on the slope. And since, during his walk, he told himself exactly how he should play his approach, how he should stand, how he should swing, he later stood and swung without destructive uncertainty, and so pitched fairly to the pin. The putt was simple; Mr. Mott achieved it without a tremor.

"Three!" he whispered to himself. "One under par! One under par for two holes! Gosh! If I hadn't been so rotten up to the fifteenth I'd have had a chance!" Aloud, he said: "Par four's too much for this hole. It ought to be three. What was yours?"

"Four," said Chapman. "Your approach was too good; it was a wonder."

"Pure wrist shot. Notice how I took the club back? Sort of scoop the ball up—pick it up clean? That's what I've been working for—pick 'em up clean with lots of back spin. You get that by sort of sliding under the ball. Well, two more to go!"

"Let's make 'em good!" adjured Chapman.

"One under par for two holes," thought Mr. Mott, slashing a low drive to the open. "Say, I guess somebody wouldn't turn up his nose at that, eh? A five and a three! I was—let's see—thirty-eight for five holes, and a five and a three make forty-six. Oh, I beg your pardon!" He was wool-gathering squarely in front of Chapman, who presently put a hooked ball somewhat beyond Mr. Mott's. "My! what a wonderful day for golf!" said Mr. Mott, enthusiastically. "Not a breath of wind, not too hot, just right."

"It suits me. You got a nice drive there."

"Too high," said Mr. Mott. He played a jumping shot which ran briskly over the shallow pit guarding the green, and came to a standstill not twenty feet from the cup. He putted, and was dead. He holed out with neatness and precision, and knew that he had beaten Chapman by a stroke. "Gad, what a green!" said Mr. Mott, pop-eyed. "Like a billiard-table. We've got an English greens-keeper here; he's a wonder. Best greenskeeper in the East. Sleepy Hollow and Pine Valley have nothing on *us!*"

"You're finishing strong, Mr. Mott. Go to it!"

"One under par for three holes," shouted Mr. Mott's dual personality to Mr. Mott. "And—how many am I to here?" To Chapman he said, "I'm trying to remember—what did I have on the tenth?"

"Six," said Chapman.

"Why, are you sure?"

"Positive."

"Well, I *thought* I remembered it was six,—I've been counting up,—but—"

"I can name every stroke you've played since you started," said Chapman. "It gets to be second nature after a while. It's only a knack; but sometimes it's very valuable. I know every shot we've *both* played."

Mr. Mott looked doubtful.

"I'd take the short end of a sizable bet on that proposition. What was my fourth shot on the fourth hole?"

"Brassey to the green," said Chapman. "You got a six."

"Well, I'll be—what did I make on the seventh hole? "

"Seven."

"Well, what was my third shot on the tenth?"

"Just a minute—why, it was a topped mashie into the trap. You were on in four and down in six."

Mr. Mott prepared to drive.

"Do you always remember scores like that?"

"Always."

Mr. Mott drove far down the fairway. Exalted and emboldened, he ventured to explain briefly just how he had done it. Then when Chapman had hit a long, low ball which developed a faint hook as it dipped to the hollows, Mr. Mott was constrained to offer condolence.

"If you just get that kink out of your shots you'll play under a hundred," he stated flatly. "Under a hundred with no trouble at all."

His companion chuckled involuntarily.

"Well, I hope I should."

"Nothing in the world but too much wrist action. Look! You don't see *me* hooking many balls, do you? Watch how I get my wrists into this one!" He was unerring on the line, and Chapman nodded understandingly.

"You couldn't ask anything better than that."

"And the best of it is," said Mr. Mott, glowing, "that I always know what's the matter with me. I wasn't always that way; there was a time when I was way up in the air about it, so I know just how you feel. Now go after this one! Easy—and follow through! Oh—too bad!"

Chapman, however, wasn't overly discouraged.

"It's safe, isn't it?"

"Yes, it's almost up on the brook; but if you'd gone into the woods, it would have been a lost ball. *This* way!" Mr. Mott illustrated once more. "Here she goes!" And he made his third consecutive shot which was without reproach.

Chapman, however, hooked a trifle even with his full mashie, which was barely off the green, and Mr. Mott sighed for him. For himself, he ran up alongside. If he could go down in two more, he would have played the last four holes in par! Mr. Mott reached for his putter, and fumbled with it. He bent over the ball, and observed that it was smaller than he had suspected; he told himself that he should have chosen a larger size. Mr. Mott's lips formed the word "Fore!" and he tapped impotently. The ball rolled in, swerved, struck a transient leaf, and Mr. Mott, his mind erased of any conception of a partner, or of the etiquette of the links, dashed forward. Two feet to the cup, two feet for a six, and the last four holes in par! Fifty-one for the last nine—his record! Mr. Mott, gasping, clutched the putter, and struck, and heard the click of the contact, and saw a cylindrical abyss, lined with zinc, open wide to receive the Silver King. He stood up, choked with emotion.

"The—last four holes in—in *par!*" he faltered.

"Hold the flag, boy!" said Chapman.

Mr. Mott watched, fascinated. Inwardly he knew, before Chapman putted, that the stroke was too light; and as the lanky stranger strolled up for further trial, Mr. Mott, in his terrific success, blurted out his final charge.

"If you don't mind my telling you," he said, "rest your right hand on your knee, and—"

The ball rattled into the cup. From a camp-chair under the awning, a member of the Board of Governors rose and sauntered toward them.

"Mr. Chapman!" said Mr. Mott. He offered his hand across the hole.

"Thank you, Mr. Mott." Chapman's clasp was convincing.

"I was par for the last four holes! If I'd only got back on my game sooner! Listen! If you didn't hook so much—"

"Yes?" The voice of the stranger was dull with weariness.

"Well, you saw what *I* did! I came back in fifty-one, and the last four in par! Why, if you can play an even game with me *now*—"

"Hello, Chap," said the Governor at his elbow. "How are you going?"

"Fine!" said Mr. Mott, answering for him. "If he only didn't hook so much! How *did* we come out? I was a hundred and fourteen, and you—"

"Eighty-one," said Chapman. "Not bad for a starter." His tone was utterly serious; he wasn't jesting.

Mr. Mott's eyes widened. His mouth sagged. A spot of color appeared above his cheek-bones.

"Why, that's impossible. That's—"

"Forty-one for first nine, and forty for the last." Mr. Mott shook as though with palsy, and the putter fell from his hands. He had ignored Chapman's medal score, but now he was recalling incident after incident which seemed to suggest that Chapman had made recoveries, and got distance, and dropped occasional putts. . . .

"Why . . . why . . . I thought we were going about even!"

"Count 'em up," said Chapman, soberly. "6, 5, 4, 5, 5, 3, 4, 4, 5; isn't that forty-one? 5, 4, 4, 2, 6, 5, 4, 5, 5; isn't that forty?"

"You—you didn't get—a two on the thirteenth!"

"Certainly I did. I holed out while you were in the pit."

Mr. Mott, now that he flogged his memory for the facts, seemed dimly to recognize that even those swerving shots of Chapman's had gone off smoothly, and that Chapman had approached sweetly, and putted with distinction. But an eighty-one! And he had volunteered to coach this man; he had showed him in detail how various shots should be made; he had claimed the privilege of instructing a stranger who had hit hardly a straight ball, and still scored close to eighty.

"Wh—what's your handicap?" he stammered. "You—you aren't *that* Chapman—are you?"

The Governor put his arm over the shoulders of the lanky stranger.

"He had three in New England," he said, "but in the Met, I suppose they'll give him four. How were *you* going, Mr. Mott?"

"Oh, pretty fair—for me," said Mr. Mott, feebly.

But when, bathed and ennobled by fresh linen, he left the clubhouse his heart was once more proud and high. Now and then, to be sure, he experienced a spasm of mortification at the ridiculous figure he had cut before Chapman; nevertheless he was sustained and soothed by the remembrance of the last nine holes in fifty-one and the last four in par. He felt a sturdy manhood, confident and unafraid. Today he had scored a hundred and fourteen; tomorrow it might be that he, too, should play the full round as he had played the last four holes today; upon such dreams is founded the wealth of the club-makers and the athletic outfitters. Timidity in the presence of hazards had gone from him, he believed, forever. Timidity on the greens was a thing of the past. If he could lower his average to a hundred and five by the end of the season,—and with four holes in par today he could conceivably do five in par next Saturday, or perhaps as many as six or seven,—he might get down to, say, ninety by next year. If a slim built Bostonian with no style to speak of could approximate eighty, why not Mr. Mott? If a man with a chronic hook could merit a four handicap, why not Mr. Mott? He saw roseate visions of himself at scratch; Walter Travis was already middle-aged before *he* took up the game.

"The last four in par!" whispered Mr. Mott as he went up the steps of his house.

"*Well,*" said Mrs. Mott, pathetically, as she came to greet him, "was it worth a thousand dollars to you, Val, to stay away *all* this lovely afternoon?"

"Every cent of it!" cried Mr. Mott, hilariously. "Say, let's motor up the road somewhere; want to? Let's have dinner out! Here, I know! We'll run up to Tumble Inn. Get the Smithsons, and we'll have a party."

"I thought you said you couldn't go out to-night!" She was frankly suspicious.

"Rot! I never said that, did I? Must have been a slip of the tongue. Call the Smithsons, will you?"

"It *must* have been worth while, your staying," said Mrs. Mott, brightening.

"Well, it was," said Mr. Mott. "And I got the last four holes in par! Hurry up and telephone!"

And as he waited for her report, the man who had played a hundred and fourteen stood before the long mirror in the hallway, and gripped an imaginary club, and swung it, and finished gloriously, with the body well twisted and the hands close to the neck, and grinned happily at the reflection of another champion in the making. For this is at once the faith and the hope, the Credo and the Te Deum of the golfer of all time and of whatever ability— Thank God for to-morrow!

CHAPTER 18

WINTER DREAMS

F. SCOTT FITZGERALD

I

Some of the caddies were poor as sin and lived in one-room houses with a neurasthenic cow in the front yard, but Dexter Green's father owned the second best grocery store in Black Bear—the best one was "The Hub," patronized by the wealthy people from Sherry Island—and Dexter caddied only for pocket money.

In the fall when the days became crisp and gray and the long Minnesota winter shut down like the white lid of a box, Dexter's skis moved over the snow that hid the fairways of the golf course. At these times the country gave him a feeling of profound melancholy—it offended him that the links should lie in enforced fallowness, haunted by ragged sparrows for the long season. It was dreary, too, that on the tees where the gay colors fluttered in summer there were now only the desolate sandboxes knee-deep in crusted ice. When he crossed the hills the wind blew cold as misery and if the sun was out he tramped with his eyes squinted up against the hard dimensionless glare.

In April the winter ceased abruptly. The snow ran down into Black Bear Lake scarcely tarrying for the early golfers to brave the season with red and black balls. Without elation, without an interval of moist glory, the cold was gone.

In the winter, the snow hid the fairways of the golf course. *(morrbyte, courtesy of iStock)*

Dexter knew that there was something dismal about this Northern spring, just as he knew there was something gorgeous about the fall. Fall made him clinch his hands and tremble and repeat idiotic sentences to himself, and make brisk abrupt gestures of command to imaginary audiences and armies. October filled him with hope which November raised to a sort of ecstatic triumph, and in this mood the fleeting brilliant impressions of the summer at Sherry Island were ready grist to his mill. He became a golf champion and defeated Mr. T. A. Hedrick in a marvelous match played a hundred times over the fairways of his imagination, a match each detail of which he changed about untiringly—sometimes he won with almost laughable ease, sometimes he came up magnificently from behind. Again, stepping from a Pierce-Arrow automobile, like Mr. Mortimer Jones, he strolled frigidly into the lounge of the Sherry Island Golf Club—or perhaps, surrounded by an admiring crowd, he gave an exhibition of fancy diving from the springboard of the club raft. . . . Among those who watched him in open-mouthed won-der was Mr. Mortimer Jones.

And one day it came to pass that Mr. Jones—himself and not his ghost—came up to Dexter with tears in his eyes and said that Dexter was the damned best caddy in the club, and wouldn't he decide not to quit if Mr. Jones made it worth his while, because every other damn caddy in the club lost one ball a hole for him—regularly—

"No, sir," said Dexter decisively. "I don't want to caddie any more." Then, after a pause: "I'm too old."

"You're not more than fourteen. Why the devil did you decide just this morning that you wanted to quit? You promised that next week you'd go over to the state tournament with me."

"I decided I was too old."

Dexter handed in his "A Class" badge, collected what money was due him from the caddy master, and walked home to Black Bear Village. "The best damned caddy I ever saw," shouted Mr. Mortimer Jones over a drink that afternoon. "Never lost a ball! Willing! Intelligent! Quiet! Honest! Grateful!"

The little girl who had done this was eleven—beautifully ugly as little girls are apt to be who are destined after a few years to be inexpressibly lovely and bring no end of misery to a great number of men. The spark, however, was perceptible. There was a general ungodliness in the way her lips twisted down at the corners when she smiled, and in the—Heaven help us!—in the almost passionate quality of her eyes. Vitality is born in such women. It was utterly in evidence now, shining through her thin frame in a sort of glow.

She had come eagerly out on to the course at nine o'clock with a white linen nurse and five small new golf-clubs in a white canvas bag which the nurse was carrying. When Dexter first saw her she was standing by the caddy house, rather ill at ease and trying to conceal the fact by engaging her nurse in an obviously unnatural conversation graced by startling and irrelevant gri-maces from herself.

"Well, it's certainly a nice day, Hilda," Dexter heard her say. She drew down the corners of her mouth, smiled, and glanced furtively around, her eyes in transit falling for an instant on Dexter.

Then to the nurse:

"Well, I guess there aren't very many people out here this morning, are there?"

The smile again—radiant, blatantly artificial—convincing.

"I don't know what we're supposed to do now," said the nurse, looking nowhere in particular.

"Oh, that's all right. I'll fix it up."

Dexter stood perfectly still, his mouth slightly ajar. He knew that if he moved forward a step his stare would be in her line of vision—if he moved backward he would lose his full view of her face. For a moment he had not realized how young she was. Now he remembered having seen her several times the year before—in bloomers.

Suddenly, involuntarily, he laughed, a short abrupt laugh—then, startled by himself, he turned and began to walk quickly away.

"Boy!"

Dexter stopped.

"Boy—"

Beyond question he was addressed. Not only that, but he was treated to that absurd smile, that preposterous smile—the memory of which at least a dozen men were to carry into middle age.

"Boy, do you know where the golf teacher is?"

"He's giving a lesson."

"Well, do you know where the caddy master is?"

"He isn't here yet this morning."

"Oh." For a moment this baffled her. She stood alternately on her right and left foot.

"We'd like to get a caddy," said the nurse. "Mrs. Mortimer Jones sent us out to play golf, and we don't know how without we get a caddy."

Here she was stopped by an ominous glance from Miss Jones, followed immediately by the smile.

"There aren't any caddies here except me," said Dexter to the nurse, "and I got to stay here in charge until the caddy master gets here."

"Oh."

Miss Jones and her retinue now withdrew, and at a proper distance from Dexter became involved in a heated conversation, which was concluded by Miss Jones taking one of the clubs and hitting it on the ground with violence. For further emphasis she raised it again and was about to bring it down smartly upon the nurse's bosom, when the nurse seized the club and twisted it from her hands.

"You damn little mean old thing!" cried Miss Jones wildly.

Another argument ensued. Realizing that the elements of the comedy were implied in the scene, Dexter several times began to laugh, but each time restrained the laugh before it reached audibility. He could not resist the monstrous conviction that the little girl was justified in beating the nurse.

The situation was resolved by the fortuitous appearance of the caddy master, who was appealed to immediately by the nurse.

"Miss Jones is to have a little caddy, and this one says he can't go."

"Mr. McKenna said I was to wait here till you came," said Dexter quickly.

"Well, he's here now." Miss Jones smiled cheerfully at the caddy master.

Then she dropped her bag and set off at a haughty mince toward the first tee.

"Well?" The caddy master turned to Dexter. "What you standing there like a dummy for? Go pick up the young lady's clubs."

"I don't think I'll go out today," said Dexter.

"You don't—"

"I think I'll quit."

The enormity of his decision frightened him. He was a favorite caddy, and the thirty dollars a month he earned through the summer were not to be made elsewhere around the lake. But he had received a strong emotional shock, and his perturbation required a violent and immediate outlet.

It is not so simple as that, either. As so frequently would be the case in the future, Dexter was unconsciously dictated to by his winter dreams.

II

Now, of course, the quality and the seasonability of these winter dreams varied, but the stuff of them remained. They persuaded Dexter several years later to pass up a business course at the state university—his father, prospering now, would have paid his way—for the precarious advantage of attending an older and more famous university in the East, where he was bothered by his scanty funds. But do not get the impression, because his winter dreams happened to be concerned at first with musings on the rich, that there was anything merely snobbish in the boy. He wanted not association with glittering things and glittering people—he wanted the glittering things themselves. Often he reached out for the best without knowing why he wanted it—and sometimes he ran up against the mysterious denials and prohibitions in which life indulges. It is with one of those denials and not with his career as a whole that this story deals.

He made money. It was rather amazing. After college he went to the city from which Black Bear Lake draws its wealthy patrons. When he was only twenty-three and had been there not quite two years, there were already people who liked to say: "Now there's a boy—"All about him rich men's sons were peddling bonds precariously or investing patrimonies precariously, or plodding through the two dozen volumes of the "George Washington Commercial Course," but Dexter borrowed a thousand dollars on his college degree and his confident mouth, and bought a partnership in a laundry.

It was a small laundry when he went into it, but Dexter made a specialty of learning how the English washed fine woolen golf stockings without shrinking them, and within a year he was catering to the trade that wore knickerbockers. Men were insisting that their Shetland hose and sweaters go to his laundry, just as they had insisted on a caddy who could find golf balls. A little later he was doing then-wives' lingerie as well—and running five branches in different parts of the city. Before he was twenty-seven he owned the largest string of laundries in his section of the country. It was then that he sold out and went to New York. But the part of his story that concerns us goes back to the days when he was making his first big success.

When he was twenty-three Mr. Hart—one of the gray-haired men who like to say, "Now there's a boy"—gave him a guest card to the Sherry Island Golf Club for a weekend. So he signed his name one day on the register, and that afternoon played golf in a foursome with Mr. Hart and Mr. Sandwood and Mr. T. A. Hedrick. He did not consider it necessary to remark that he had once carried Mr. Hart's bag over this same links, and that he knew every trap and gully with his eyes shut—but he found himself glancing at the four caddies who trailed them, trying to catch a gleam or gesture that would remind him of himself, that would lessen the gap which lay between his present and his past.

It was a curious day slashed abruptly with fleeting, familiar impressions. One minute he had the sense of being a trespasser—in the next he was impressed by the tremendous superiority he felt toward Mr. T. A. Hedrick, who was a bore and not even a good golfer any more.

Then, because of a ball Mr. Hart lost near the fifteenth green, an enormous thing happened. While they were searching the stiff grasses of the rough there was a clear call of "Fore!" from behind a hill in their rear. And as they all turned abruptly from their search a bright new ball sliced abruptly over the hill and caught Mr. T. A. Hedrick in the abdomen.

"By Gad!" cried Mr. T. A. Hedrick, "they ought to put some of these crazy women off the course. It's getting to be outrageous."

A head and a voice came up together over the hill:

"Do you mind if we go through?"

"You hit me in the stomach!" declared Mr. Hedrick wildly.

"Did I?" The girl approached the group of men. "I'm sorry. I yelled, 'Fore!'"

Her glance fell casually on each of the men—then scanned the fairway for her ball.

"Did I bounce into the rough?"

It was impossible to determine whether this question was ingenuous or malicious. In a moment, however, she left no doubt, for as her partner came up over the hill she called cheerfully:

"Here I am! I'd have gone on the green except that I hit something."

As she took her stance for a short mashie shot, Dexter looked at her closely. She wore a blue gingham dress, rimmed at throat and shoulders with a white edging that accentuated her tan. The quality of exaggeration, of thinness, which had made her passionate eyes and down-turning mouth absurd at eleven, was gone now. She was arrestingly beautiful. The color in her cheeks was centered like the color in a picture—it was not a "high" color, but a sort of fluctuating and feverish warmth, so shaded that it seemed at any moment it would recede and disappear. This color and the mobility of her mouth gave a continual impression of flux, of intense life, of passionate vitality—balanced only partially by the sad luxury of her eyes.

She swung her mashie impatiently and without interest, pitching the ball into a sand pit on the other side of the green. With a quick, insincere smile and a careless "Thank you!" she went on after it.

"That Judy Jones!" remarked Mr. Hedrick on the next tee, as they waited—some moments—for her to play on ahead. "All she needs is to be turned

She swung her mashie impatiently and without interest, pitching the ball into a sand pit on the other side of the green. *(ansonsaw, courtesy of iStock)*

up and spanked for six months and then to be married off to an old-fashioned cavalry captain."

"My God, she's good-looking!" said Mr. Sandwood, who was just over thirty.

"Good-looking!" cried Mr. Hedrick contemptuously. "She always looks as if she wanted to be kissed! Turning those big cow eyes on every calf in town!"

It was doubtful if Mr. Hedrick intended a reference to the maternal instinct.

"She'd play pretty good golf if she'd try," said Mr. Sandwood.

"She has no form," said Mr. Hedrick solemnly.

"She has a nice figure," said Mr. Sandwood.

"Better thank the Lord she doesn't drive a swifter ball," said Mr. Hart, winking at Dexter.

Later in the afternoon the sun went down with a swirl of gold and varying blues and scarlets, and left the dry, rustling night of Western summer. Dexter watched from the veranda of the golf club, watched the even overlap of the waters in the little wind, silver molasses under the harvest moon. Then the moon held a finger to her lips and the lake became a clear pool, pale and quiet. Dexter put on his bathing suit and swam out to the farthest raft, where he stretched dripping on the wet canvas of the springboard.

There was a fish jumping and a star shining and the lights around the lake were gleaming. Over on a dark peninsula a piano was playing the songs of last summer and of summers before that—songs from "Chin-Chin" and "The Count of Luxembourg" and "The Chocolate Soldier"—and because the sound of a piano over a stretch of water had always seemed beautiful to Dexter he lay perfectly quiet and listened.

The tune the piano was playing at that moment had been gay and new five years before when Dexter was a sophomore at college. They had played it at a prom once when he could not afford the luxury of proms, and he had stood outside the gymnasium and listened. The sound of the tune precipitated in him a sort of ecstasy and it was with that ecstasy he viewed what happened to him now. It was a mood of intense appreciation, a sense that, for once, he was magnificently attuned to life and that everything about him was radiating brightness and a glamor he might never know again.

A low, pale oblong detached itself suddenly from the darkness of the island, spitting forth the reverberate sound of a racing motorboat. Two white streamers of cleft water rolled themselves out behind it and almost immediately the boat was beside him, drowning out the hot tinkle of the piano in the drone of its spray. Dexter raising himself on his arms was aware of a figure standing at the wheel, of two dark eyes regarding him over the lengthening space of water—then the boat had gone by and was sweeping in an immense and purposeless circle of spray round and round in the middle of the lake. With equal eccentricity one of the circles flattened out and headed back toward the raft.

"Who's that?" she called, shutting off her motor. She was so near now that Dexter could see her bathing suit, which consisted apparently of pink rompers.

The nose of the boat bumped the raft, and as the latter tilted rakishly he was precipitated toward her. With different degrees of interest they recognized each other.

"Aren't you one of those men we played through this afternoon?" she demanded.

He was.

"Well, do you know how to drive a motorboat? Because if you do I wish you'd drive this one so I can ride on the surfboard behind. My name is Judy Jones"—she favored him with an absurd smirk—rather, what tried to be a smirk, for, twist her mouth as she might, it was not grotesque, it was merely beautiful—"and I live in a house over there on the island, and in that house there is a man waiting for me. When he drove up at the door I drove out of the dock because he says I'm his ideal."

There was a fish jumping and a star shining and the lights around the lake were gleaming. Dexter sat beside Judy Jones and she explained how her boat was driven. Then she was in the water, swimming to the floating surfboard with a sinuous crawl. Watching her was without effort to the eye, watching a branch waving or a sea gull flying. Her arms, burned to butternut, moved sinuously among the dull platinum ripples, elbow appearing first, casting the forearm back with a cadence of falling water, then reaching out and down, stabbing a path ahead.

They moved out into the lake: turning, Dexter saw that she was kneeling on the low rear of the now uptilted surfboard.

"Go faster," she called, "fast as it'll go."

Obediently he jammed the lever forward and the white spray mounted at the bow. When he looked around again the girl was standing up on the rushing board, her arms spread wide, her eyes lifted toward the moon.

"It's awful cold," she shouted. "What's your name?"

He told her.

"Well, why don't you come to dinner tomorrow night?"

His heart turned over like the flywheel of the boat, and, for the second time, her casual whim gave a new direction to his life.

III

Next evening while he waited for her to come downstairs, Dexter peopled the soft deep summer room and the sun porch that opened from it with the men who had already loved Judy Jones. He knew the sort of men they were—the men who when he first went to college had entered from the great prep schools with graceful clothes and the deep tan of healthy summers. He had seen that, in one sense, he was better than these men. He was newer and stronger. Yet in acknowledging to himself that he wished his children to be like them he was admitting that he was but the rough, strong stuff from which they eternally sprang.

When the time had come for him to wear good clothes, he had known who were the best tailors in America, and the best tailors in America had made him the suit he wore this evening. He had acquired that particular reserve peculiar to his university that set it off from other universities. He recognized the value to him of such a mannerism and he had adopted it; he knew that to be careless in dress and manner required more confidence than to be careful. But carelessness was for his children. His mother's name had been Krimplich. She was a Bohemian of the peasant class and she had talked broken English to the end of her days. Her son must keep to the set patterns.

At a little after seven Judy Jones came downstairs. She wore a blue silk afternoon dress, and he was disappointed at first that she had not put on something more elaborate. This feeling was accentuated when, after a brief greeting, she went to the door of a butler's pantry and pushing it open called: "You can serve dinner, Martha." He had rather expected that a butler would announce dinner, that there would be a cocktail. Then he put these thoughts behind him as they sat down side by side on a lounge and looked at each other.

"Father and mother won't be here," she said thoughtfully.

He remembered the last time he had seen her father, and he was glad the parents were not to be here tonight—they might wonder who he was. He had been born in Keeble, a Minnesota village fifty miles farther north, and he always gave Keeble as his home instead of Black Bear Village. Country towns were well enough to come from if they weren't inconveniently in sight and used as footstools by fashionable lakes.

They talked of his university, which she had visited frequently during the past two years, and of the nearby city which supplied Sherry Island with its patrons, and whither Dexter would return next day to his prospering laundries.

During dinner she slipped into a moody depression which gave Dexter a feeling of uneasiness. Whatever petulance she uttered in her throaty voice worried him. Whatever she smiled at—at him, at a chicken liver, at nothing—it disturbed him that her smile could have no root in mirth, or even in amusement. When the scarlet corners of her lips curved down, it was less a smile than an invitation to a kiss.

Then, after dinner, she led him out on the dark sun porch and deliberately changed the atmosphere.

"Do you mind if I weep a little?" she said.

"I'm afraid I'm boring you," he responded quickly.

"You're not. I like you. But I've just had a terrible afternoon. There was a man I cared about, and this afternoon he told me out of a clear sky that he was poor as a churchmouse. He'd never even hinted it before. Does this sound horribly mundane?"

"Perhaps he was afraid to tell you."

"Suppose he was," she answered. "He didn't start right. You see, if I'd thought of him as poor—well, I've been mad about loads of poor men, and fully intended to marry them all. But in this case, I hadn't thought of him that way, and my interest in him wasn't strong enough to survive the shock. As if a girl calmly informed her fiancé that she was a widow. He might not object to widows, but—

"Let's start right," she interrupted herself suddenly. "Who are you, anyhow?"

For a moment Dexter hesitated. Then: "I'm nobody," he announced.

"My career is largely a matter of futures."

"Are you poor?"

"No," he said frankly. "I'm probably making more money than any man my age in the Northwest. I know that's an obnoxious remark, but you advised me to start right."

There was a pause. Then she smiled and the corners of her mouth drooped and an almost imperceptible sway brought her closer to him, looking up into his eyes. A lump rose in Dexter's throat, and he waited breathless for the experiment, facing the unpredictable compound that would form mysteriously from the elements of their lips. Then he saw—she communicated her excitement to him, lavishly, deeply, with kisses that were not a promise but a fulfillment. They aroused in him not hunger demanding renewal but surfeit that would demand more surfeit . . . kisses that were like charity creating want by holding back nothing at all.

It did not take him many hours to decide that he had wanted Judy Jones ever since he was a proud, desirous little boy.

IV

It began like that—and continued, with varying shades of intensity on such a note right up to the dénouement. Dexter surrendered a part of himself to the most direct and unprincipled personality with which he had ever come in contact. Whatever Judy wanted, she went after with the full pressure of her charm. There was no divergence of method, no jockeying for position or premeditation of effects—there was a very little mental side to any of her affairs. She simply made men conscious to the highest degree of her physical loveliness. Dexter had no desire to change her. Her deficiencies were knit up with a passionate energy that transcended and justified them.

When, as Judy's head lay against his shoulder that first night, she whispered, "I don't know what's the matter with me. Last night I thought I was in love with a man and tonight I think I'm in love with you—" It seemed to him a beautiful and romantic thing to say. It was the exquisite excitability that for the moment he controlled and owned. But a week later he was compelled to view this same quality in a different light. She took him in her roadster to a picnic supper, and after supper she disappeared, likewise in her roadster, with another man. Dexter became enormously upset and was scarcely able to be decently civil to the other people present. When she assured him that she had not kissed the other man, he knew she was lying—yet he was glad that she had taken the trouble to lie to him.

He was, as he found before the summer ended, one of a varying dozen who circulated about her. Each of them had at one time been favored above all others—about half of them still basked in the solace of occasional sentimental revivals. Whenever one showed signs of dropping out through long neglect, she granted him a brief honeyed hour, which encouraged him to tag along for a year or so longer. Judy made these forays upon the helpless and defeated without malice, indeed half unconscious that there was anything mischievous in what she did.

When a new man came to town every one dropped out—dates were automatically canceled.

The helpless part of trying to do anything about it was that she did it all herself. She was not a girl who could be "won" in the kinetic sense—she was proof against cleverness, she was proof against charm: if any of these assailed her too strongly she would immediately resolve the affair to a physical basis, and under the magic of her physical splendor the strong as well as the brilliant played her game and not their own. She was entertained only by the gratification of her desires and by the direct exercise of her own charm. Perhaps from so much youthful love, so many youthful lovers, she had come, in self-defense, to nourish herself wholly from within.

Succeeding Dexter's first exhilaration came restlessness and dissatisfaction. The helpless ecstasy of losing himself in her was opiate rather than tonic. It was fortunate for his work during the winter that those moments of ecstasy came infrequently. Early in their acquaintance it had seemed for a while that there was a deep and spontaneous mutual attraction—that first August, for example—three days of long evenings on her dusky veranda, of strange wan kisses through the late afternoon, in shadowy alcoves or behind the protecting trellises of the garden arbors, of mornings when she was fresh as a dream and almost shy at meeting him in the clarity of the rising day. There was all the ecstasy of an engagement about it, sharpened by his realization that there was no engagement. It was during those three days that, for the first time, he had asked her to marry him. She said, "Maybe someday." She said, "Kiss me." She said, "I'd like to marry you." She said, "I love you"—she said—nothing.

The three days were interrupted by the arrival of a New York man who visited at her house for half September. To Dexter's agony rumor engaged them. The man was the son of the president of a great trust company. But at the end of a month it was reported that Judy was yawning. At a dance one night she sat all evening in a motorboat with a local beau, while the New Yorker searched the club for her frantically. She told the local beau that she was bored with her visitor, and two days later he left. She was seen with him at the station, and it was reported that he looked very mournful indeed.

On this note the summer ended. Dexter was twenty-four, and he found himself increasingly in a position to do as he wished. He joined two clubs in the city and lived at one of them. Though he was by no means an integral part of the stag lines at these clubs, he managed to be on hand at dances where Judy Jones was likely to appear. He could have gone out socially as much as he liked—he was an eligible young man, now, and popular with downtown fathers. His confessed devotion to Judy Jones had rather solidified his position. But he had no social aspirations and rather despised the dancing men who were always on tap for the Thursday or Saturday parties and who filled in at dinners with the younger married set. Already he was playing with the idea of going East to New York. He wanted to take Judy Jones with him. No disillusion as to the world in which she had grown up could cure his illusion as to her desirability.

Remember that—for only in the light of it can what he did for her be understood.

Eighteen months after he first met Judy Jones he became engaged to another girl. Her name was Irene Scheerer, and her father was one of the men who had always believed in Dexter. Irene was light-haired and sweet and honorable, and a little stout, and she had two suitors whom she pleasantly relinquished when Dexter formally asked her to marry him.

Summer, fall, winter, spring, another summer, another fall—so much he had given of his active life to the incorrigible lips of Judy Jones. She had treated him with interest, with encouragement, with malice, with indifference, with contempt. She had inflicted on him the innumerable little slights and indignities possible in such a case—as if in revenge for having ever cared for him at all. She had beckoned him and yawned at him and beckoned him again and he had responded often with bitterness and narrowed eyes. She had brought him ecstatic happiness and intolerable agony of spirit. She had caused him untold inconvenience and not a little trouble. She had insulted him, and she had ridden over him, and she had played his interest in her against his interest in his work—for fun. She had done everything to him except to criticize him—this she had not done—it seemed to him only because it might have sullied the utter indifference she manifested and sincerely felt toward him.

When autumn had come and gone again it occurred to him that he could not have Judy Jones. He had to beat this into his mind but he convinced himself at last. He lay awake at night for a while and argued it over. He told himself the trouble and the pain she had caused him, he enumerated her glaring deficiencies as a wife. Then he said to himself that he loved her, and after a while he fell asleep. For a week, lest he imagine her husky voice over the telephone or her eyes opposite him at lunch, he worked hard and late, and at night he went to his office and plotted out his years.

At the end of a week he went to a dance and cut in on her once. For almost the first time since they had met he did not ask her to sit out with him or tell her that she was lovely. It hurt him that she did not miss these things—that was all. He was not jealous when he saw that there was a new man tonight. He had been hardened against jealousy long before.

He stayed late at the dance. He sat for an hour with Irene Scheerer and talked about books and about music. He knew very little about either. But he was beginning to be master of his own time now, and he had a rather priggish notion that he—the young and already fabulously successful Dexter Green—should know more about such things.

That was in October, when he was twenty-five. In January, Dexter and Irene became engaged. It was to be announced in June, and they were to be married three months later.

The Minnesota winter prolonged itself interminably, and it was almost May when the winds came soft and the snow ran down into Black Bear Lake at last. For the first time in over a year Dexter was enjoying a certain tranquility of spirit. Judy Jones had been in Florida, and afterward in Hot Springs, and somewhere she had been engaged, and somewhere she had broken it off. At first, when Dexter had definitely given her up, it had made him sad that people still linked them together and asked for news of her, but when he began to be placed at dinner next to Irene Scheerer people didn't ask him about her any more—they told him about her. He ceased to be an authority on her.

May at last. Dexter walked the streets at night when the darkness was damp as rain, wondering that so soon, with so little done, so much of ecstasy had gone from him. May one year back had been marked by Judy's poignant, unforgivable, yet forgiven turbulence—it had been one of those rare times when he fancied she had grown to care for him. That old penny's worth of happiness he had spent for this bushel of content. He knew that Irene would be no more than a curtain spread behind him, a hand moving among gleaming teacups, a voice calling to children . . . fire and loveliness were gone, the magic of nights and the wonder of the varying hours and seasons . . . slender lips, down-turning, dropping to his lips and bearing him up into a heaven of eyes. . . . The thing was deep in him. He was too strong and alive for it to die lightly.

In the middle of May when the weather balanced for a few days on the thin bridge that led to deep summer he turned in one night at Irene's house. Their engagement was to be announced in a week now—no one would be surprised at it. And tonight they would sit together on the lounge at the University Club and look on for an hour at the dancers. It gave him a sense of solidity to go with her—she was so sturdily popular, so intensely "great."

He mounted the steps of the brownstone house and stepped inside.

"Irene," he called.

Mrs. Scheerer came out of the living room to meet him.

"Dexter," she said. "Irene's gone upstairs with a splitting headache.

"She wanted to go with you, but I made her go to bed."

"Nothing serious, I—"

"Oh, no. She's going to play golf with you in the morning. You can spare her for just one night, can't you, Dexter?"

Her smile was kind. She and Dexter liked each other. In the living room he talked for a moment before he said good night.

Returning to the University Club, where he had rooms, he stood in the doorway for a moment and watched the dancers. He leaned against the door post, nodded at a man or two—yawned.

"Hello, darling."

The familiar voice at his elbow startled him. Judy Jones had left a man and crossed the room to him—Judy Jones, a slender enameled doll in cloth of gold: gold in a band at her head, gold in two slipper points at her dress's hem. The fragile glow of her face seemed to blossom as she smiled, at him. A breeze of warmth and light blew through the room.

His hands in the pockets of his dinner jacket tightened spasmodically. He was filled with a sudden excitement.

"When did you get back?" he asked casually.

"Come here and I'll tell you about it."

She turned and he followed her. She had been away—he could have wept at the wonder of her return. She had passed through enchanted streets, doing things that were like provocative music. All mysterious happenings, all fresh and quickening hopes, had gone away with her, come back with her now.

She turned in the doorway.

"Have you a car here? If you haven't, I have."

"I have a coupé."

In then, with a rustle of golden cloth. He slammed the door. Into so many cars she had stepped—like this—like that—her back against the leather, so—her elbow resting on the door—waiting. She would have been soiled long since had there been anything to soil her—except herself—but this was her own self outpouring.

With an effort he forced himself to start the car and back into the street. This was nothing, he must remember. She had done this before, and he had put her behind him, as he would have crossed a bad account from his books.

He drove slowly downtown and, affecting abstraction, traversed the deserted streets of the business section, peopled here and there where a movie was giving out its crowd or where consumptive or pugilistic youth lounged in front of pool halls. The clink of glasses and the slap of hands on the bars issued from saloons, cloisters of glazed glass and dirty yellow light.

She was watching him closely and the silence was embarrassing, yet in this crisis he could find no casual word with which to profane the hour. At a convenient turning he began to zigzag back toward the University Club.

"Have you missed me?" she asked suddenly.

"Everybody missed you."

He wondered if she knew of Irene Scheerer. She had been back only a day—her absence had been almost contemporaneous with his engagement.

"What a remark!" Judy laughed sadly—without sadness. She looked at him searchingly. He became absorbed in the dashboard.

"You're handsomer than you used to be," she said thoughtfully. "Dexter, you have the most rememberable eyes."

He could have laughed at this, but he did not laugh. It was the sort of thing that was said to sophomores. Yet it stabbed at him.

"I'm awfully tired of everything, darling." She called everyone darling, endowing the endearment with careless, individual camaraderie. "I wish you'd marry me."

The directness of this confused him. He should have told her now that he was going to marry another girl, but he could not tell her. He could as easily have sworn that he had never loved her.

"I think we'd get along," she continued on the same note, "unless probably you've forgotten me and fallen in love with another girl."

Her confidence was obviously enormous. She had said, in effect, that she found such a thing impossible to believe, that if it were true he had merely committed a childish indiscretion—and probably to show off. She would forgive him, because it was not a matter of any moment but rather something to be brushed aside lightly.

"Of course you could never love anybody but me," she continued. "I like the way you love me. Oh, Dexter, have you forgotten last year?"

"No, I haven't forgotten."

"Neither have I!"

Was she sincerely moved—or was she carried along by the wave of her own acting?

"I wish we could be like that again," she said, and he forced himself to answer:

"I don't think we can."

"I suppose not. . . . I hear you're giving Irene Scheerer a violent rush."

There was not the faintest emphasis on the name, yet Dexter was suddenly ashamed.

"Oh, take me home," cried Judy suddenly: "I don't want to go back to that idiotic dance—with those children."

Then, as he turned up the street that led to the residence district, Judy began to cry quietly to herself. He had never seen her cry before.

The dark street lightened, the dwellings of the rich loomed up around them, he stopped his coupé in front of the great white bulk of the Mortimer Joneses' house, somnolent, gorgeous, drenched with the splendor of the damp moonlight. Its solidity startled him. The strong walls, the steel of the girders, the breadth and beam and pomp of it were there only to bring out the contrast with the young beauty beside him. It was sturdy to accentuate her slightness— as if to show what a breeze could be generated by a butterfly's wing.

He sat perfectly quiet, his nerves in wild clamor, afraid that if he moved he would find her irresistibly in his arms. Two tears had rolled down her wet face and trembled on her upper lip.

"I'm more beautiful than anybody else," she said brokenly. "Why can't I be happy?" Her moist eyes tore at his stability—her mouth turned slowly downward with an exquisite sadness: "I'd like to marry you if you'll have me, Dexter. I suppose you think I'm not worth having, but I'll be so beautiful for you, Dexter."

A million phrases of anger, pride, passion, hatred, tenderness fought on his lips. Then a perfect wave of emotion washed over him, carrying off with it a sediment of wisdom, of convention, of doubt, of honor. This was his girl who was speaking, his own, his beautiful, his pride.

"Won't you come in?" He heard her draw in her breath sharply.

Waiting.

"All right," his voice was trembling. "I'll come in."

V

It was strange that neither when it was over nor a long time afterward did he regret that night. Looking at it from the perspective of ten years, the fact that Judy's flare for him endured just one month seemed of little importance. Nor did it matter that by his yielding he subjected himself to a deeper agony in the end and gave serious hurt to Irene Scheerer and to Irene's parents, who had befriended him. There was nothing sufficiently pictorial about Irene's grief to stamp itself on his mind.

Dexter was at bottom hard-minded. The attitude of the city on his action was of no importance to him, not because he was going to leave the city but because any outside attitude on the situation seemed superficial. He was completely indifferent to popular opinion. Nor, when he had seen that it was no use, that he did not possess in himself the power to move fundamentally or to hold Judy Jones, did he bear any malice toward her. He loved her, and he would love her until the day he was too old for loving but he could not have her. So he tasted the deep pain that is reserved only for the strong, just as he had tasted for a little while the deep happiness.

Even the ultimate falsity of the grounds upon which Judy terminated the engagement that she did not want to "take him away" from Irene—Judy who had wanted nothing else—did not revolt him. He was beyond any revulsion or any amusement.

He went East in February with the intention of selling out his laundries and settling in New York—but the war came to America in March and changed his plans. He returned to the West, handed over the management of the business to his partner, and went into the first officers' training camp in late April. He was one of those young thousands who greeted the war with a certain amount of relief, welcoming the liberation from webs of tangled emotion.

VI

This story is not his biography, remember, although things creep into it which have nothing to do with those dreams he had when he was young. We are almost done with them and with him now. There is only one more incident to be related here, and it happens seven years farther on.

It took place in New York, where he had done well—so well that there were no barriers too high for him. He was thirty-two years old, and, except for one flying trip immediately after the war, he had not been West in seven years. A man named Devlin from Detroit came into his office to see him in a business way, and then and there this incident occurred, and closed out, so to speak, this particular side of his life.

"So you're from the Middle West," said the man Devlin with careless curiosity. "That's funny—I thought men like you were probably born and raised on Wall Street. You know—wife of one of my best friends in Detroit came from your city. I was an usher at the wedding."

Dexter waited with no apprehension of what was coming.

"Judy Simms," said Devlin with no particular interest: "Judy Jones she was once."

"Yes, I knew her." A dull impatience spread over him. He had heard, of course, that she was married—perhaps deliberately he had heard no more.

"Awfully nice girl," brooded Devlin meaninglessly, "I'm sort of sorry for her."

"Why?" Something in Dexter was alert, receptive, at once.

"Oh, Lud Simms has gone to pieces in a way. I don't mean he ill-uses her, but he drinks and runs around—"

"Doesn't she run around?"

"No. Stays at home with her kids."

"Oh."

"She's a little too old for him," said Devlin.

"Too old!" cried Dexter. "Why, man, she's only twenty-seven."

He was possessed with a wild notion of rushing out into the streets and taking a train to Detroit. He rose to his feet spasmodically.

"I guess you're busy," Devlin apologized quickly. "I didn't realize—"

"No, I'm not busy," said Dexter, steadying his voice. "I'm not busy at all. Not busy at all. Did you say she was—twenty-seven? No, I said she was twenty-seven."

"Yes, you did," agreed Devlin dryly.

"Go on, then. Go on."

"What do you mean?"

"About Judy Jones."

Devlin looked at him helplessly.

"Well, that's—I told you all there is to it. He treats her like the devil. Oh, they're not going to get divorced or anything. When he's particularly outrageous she forgives him. In fact, I'm inclined to think she loves him. She was a pretty girl when she first came to Detroit."

A pretty girl! The phrase struck Dexter as ludicrous.

"Isn't she—a pretty girl, any more?"

"Oh, she's all right."

"Look here," said Dexter, sitting down suddenly. "I don't understand. You say she was a 'pretty girl' and now you say she's 'all right.' I don't understand what you mean—Judy Jones wasn't a pretty girl, at all. She was a great beauty. Why, I knew her. I knew her. She was—"

Devlin laughed pleasantly.

"I'm not trying to start a row," he said. "I think Judy's a nice girl and I like her. I can't understand how a man like Lud Simms could fall madly in love with her, but he did." Then he added: "Most of the women like her."

Dexter looked closely at Devlin, thinking wildly that there must be a reason for this, some insensitivity in the man or some private malice.

"Lots of women fade just like *that*," Devlin snapped his fingers. "You must have seen it happen. Perhaps I've forgotten how pretty she was at her wedding. I've seen her so much since then, you see. She has nice eyes."

A sort of dullness settled down upon Dexter. For the first time in his life he felt like getting very drunk. He knew that he was laughing loudly at something Devlin had said, but he did not know what it was or why it was funny. When, in a few minutes, Devlin went he lay down on his lounge and looked out the window at the New York sky-line into which the sun was sinking in dull lovely shades of pink and gold.

He had thought that having nothing else to lose he was invulnerable at last—but he knew that he had just lost something more, as surely as if he had married Judy Jones and seen her fade away before his eyes.

The dream was gone. Something had been taken from him. In a sort of panic he pushed the palms of his hands into his eyes and tried to bring up a picture of the waters lapping on Sherry Island and the moonlit veranda, and gingham on the golf-links and the dry sun and the gold color of her neck's soft down. And her mouth damp to his kisses and her eyes plaintive with melancholy and her freshness like new fine linen in the morning.

Why, these things were no longer in the world! They had existed and they existed no longer.

For the first time in years the tears were streaming down his face. But they were for himself now. He did not care about mouth and eyes and moving hands. He wanted to care, and he could not care. For he had gone away and he could never go back any more. The gates were closed, the sun was gone down, and there was no beauty but the gray beauty of steel that withstands all time. Even the grief he could have borne was left behind in the country of illusion, of youth, of the richness of life, where his winter dreams had flourished.

"Long ago," he said, "long ago, there was something in me, but now that thing is gone. Now that thing is gone, that thing is gone. I cannot cry I cannot care. That thing will come back no more."

BIBLIOGRAPHY

Barrett, David. *Making the Masters: Bobby Jones and the Birth of America's Greatest Golf Tournament*. New York: Skyhorse, 2012.

Bowden, Tripp. *Freddie & Me: Life Lessons from Freddie Bennett, Augusta National's Legendary Caddy Master*. New York: Skyhorse, 2009.

Fitzgerald, F. Scott. "Winter Dreams." New York: *Metropolitan Magazine*, 1922.

Hall, Holworthy. *Dormie One: and Other Golf Stories*. New York: The Century Co., 1917.

Leitch, Cecil. *Golf*. Philadelphia: J.B. Lippincott Company, 1922.

Miller, Jeff. *Grown at Glen Garden: Ben Hogan, Byron Nelson, and the Little Texas Golf Course that Propelled Them to Stardom*. New York: Skyhorse, 2012.

Ouimet, Francis. *Golf Facts for Young People*. New York: The Century Co., 1921.

Player, Gary. *Don't Choke: A Champion's Guide to Winning Under Pressure*. New York: Skyhorse, 2010.

Sabino, John. *How to Play the World's Most Exclusive Golf Clubs: A Journey Through Pine Valley, Royal Melbourne, Augusta, Muirfield, and More*. New York: Skyhorse, 2016.

Silverman, Matthew. *Golf Miscellany: Everything You Always Wanted to Know About Golf*. New York: Skyhorse, 2012.

Steele, Chester K. *The Golf Course Mystery*. Cleveland: George Scully and Company, 1919.

Sutphen, W.G. Van T. *The Golficide and other Tales of the Fair Green*. New York: Harper & Brothers, 1898.

Travers, Jerome Dunstan. *Travers' Golf Book*. New York: The Macmillan Company, 1913.

Vardon, Harry. *The Complete Golfer*. New York: McClure, Phillips & Co., 1905.

Wodehouse, P.G. *The Man Upstairs and Other Stories*. New York: Penguin, 1914.